Cambridge E

T0277176

Elements in Americ...
edited by
Francis E. Lee
Princeton University

CONVERGING ON TRUTH

*A Dynamic Perspective on Factual
Debates in American Public Opinion*

James A. Stimson

The University of North Carolina at Chapel Hill

Emily M. Wager

The University of North Carolina at Chapel Hill

CAMBRIDGE
UNIVERSITY PRESS

CAMBRIDGE
UNIVERSITY PRESS

University Printing House, Cambridge CB2 8BS, United Kingdom

One Liberty Plaza, 20th Floor, New York, NY 10006, USA

477 Williamstown Road, Port Melbourne, VIC 3207, Australia

314–321, 3rd Floor, Plot 3, Splendor Forum, Jasola District Centre, New Delhi – 110025, India

79 Anson Road, #06–04/06, Singapore 079906

Cambridge University Press is part of the University of Cambridge.

It furthers the University's mission by disseminating knowledge in the pursuit of education, learning, and research at the highest international levels of excellence.

www.cambridge.org
Information on this title: www.cambridge.org/9781108819794
DOI: 10.1017/9781108876865

First published 2020

A catalogue record for this publication is available from the British Library.

ISBN 978-1-108-81979-4 Paperback
ISBN 978-1-108-87686-5 Online
ISSN 2515-1606 (online)
ISSN 2515-1592 (print)

Converging on Truth

A Dynamic Perspective on Factual Debates in American Public Opinion

Elements in American Politics

DOI: 10.1017/9781108876865
First published online: March 2020

James A. Stimson
The University of North Carolina at Chapel Hill

Emily M. Wager
The University of North Carolina at Chapel Hill

Author for correspondence: James Stimson, jstimson@ad.unc.edu

Abstract: Much of the science of public opinion focuses on individuals, asking if they perceive or misperceive and why. This science will often emphasize the misperception and the psychological processes that produce it. But political debates have outcomes in the aggregate. In this Element, we turn to a more system-level approach, emphasizing the beliefs of whole electorates and examining facts through a dynamic lens. We argue that public opinion will converge toward the facts over time. We find that often correct views of the facts grow stronger under information flow while misperception recedes. There are cases, however, where information flow does not lead the public toward facts.

Keywords: Public Opinion, Facts, Macropolitics, Bayesian Updating

ISBNs: 9781108819794 (PB), 9781108876865 (OC)
ISSNs: 2515-1606 (online), 2515-1592 (print)

Contents

Preface: The 1980 Debate

Next Tuesday is election day. Next Tuesday all of you will go to the polls, you will stand there and make a decision. I think when you make that decision, it might be well if you would ask yourself: Are you better off than you were four years ago? Is it easier for you to go and buy things in the stores than it was four years ago? Is there more or less unemployment in the Country than there was four years ago? Is America as respected throughout the world as it was? Do you feel that our security is as safe, that we are as strong as we were four years ago? And if you answer all those questions, "Yes," why then I think your choice is very obvious as to who you will vote for [nods toward Jimmy Carter]. If you don't agree, if you don't think that this course that we have been on for the last four years is what you would like to see us follow for the next four, then I can suggest another choice that you have.

(Ronald Reagan, October 29, 1980, from his closing summary)

When those words were uttered one week before voters went to the polls, Ronald Reagan and Jimmy Carter were nearly tied in the polls. The verdict just a few days later was a ten-point near-landslide win for Reagan, one of the biggest shifts in electoral history. While it would be overly simple to attribute all of that shift to the Reagan statement, most observers, then and now, think that it was influential. If this statement did have such an impact, why?

In all of the back and forth of a presidential campaign and debate, there are countless claims and counterclaims. It is the sort of thing candidates for office say all the time. Let us examine Reagan's questions.[1] The "Are you better off" was defined by three sub-questions. The first, easier to buy things in the stores, had an obvious answer, no. The inflation rate in October 1980 was an astounding 12.3 percent (rising from 5.5 percent when Carter was elected four years earlier). The second, more or less unemployment, was a wash, 0.2 points lower than four years earlier. But it was up by 37.5 percent (7.5 compared to 5.6) over the past eighteen months, which would have been strikingly fresh in voters' memory. And the third, is our security as safe, came after a year of frustrating impotence and failure in the matter of American diplomats held hostage in Iran.

What all three questions in this example case have in common is that there were factually correct answers to Reagan's questions. Excepting the four-year frame on the unemployment issue, they were all bad news for Carter. The lesson we draw from this example is this: political rhetoric that makes factual claims is more forceful if those claims are factually true. At one level, this would seem obvious; it is better to have a positive case. But the emphasis of analysis of

---

[1] As part of a formal closing statement, both Carter's and Reagan's remarks would have been carefully crafted in advance and delivered, almost verbatim, from a script. Candidate Reagan was of course a career professional in the business of learning and delivering lines.

political rhetoric is on trickery and artifice. We tend to think that politicians succeed in persuasion because they are persuasive, skilled in the political arts. We tend to think that voters cling to untruths to hold a consistent map of partisan views. We wish to emphasize an overlooked dimension of perception and persuasion, the simple truth of the case.

Notice that Reagan's words were believed, not just by Reagan's fellow Republican partisans but also by very large proportions of all Americans, including those who opposed Ronald Reagan's candidacy. Inflation was in fact as bad as it had ever been in postwar America. Everyone knew it. The uptick in unemployment resulted from the first ever election year recession. You needn't have been a Reagan supporter or a Republican to believe that the American economy was sour at the time of the debate. The unease is obvious in consumer surveys at the time. We will document the accuracy of economic perceptions in the Element to follow.

Respect for America in the world was a much more subjective matter, one for which there was no satisfactory indicator. But the frustration of Jimmy Carter with the Iranian clerics was palpable, an out of control situation that frequently led the nightly news.

If, in fact, the accuracy of Reagan's claims explained some of the movement from a too-close-to-call squeaker to the near landslide that was the 1980 election outcome, then it illustrates a more important point, the central claim of this Element, that mass electorates process factual claims and tend to move their average beliefs about them in the direction of the truth over time. That is the case we will make in the sections to follow.

How is the economy doing? Who will win the coming election? Is the Earth warming? Is crime on the rise or decline? Are childhood vaccinations safe? These are the sorts of questions of everyday politics. Voters are exposed to views on them, sometimes consensual and sometimes contrasting. What average Americans believe about questions like these can sometimes be ascertained from public opinion surveys. Where possible, we will explore these data toward a common question that runs through them all: Do facts have leverage on opinion over time?

Much of the science of public opinion focuses on individuals, asking if they perceive or misperceive and why. Pretty often this science will emphasize the misperception and the psychological processes that produce it. But political debates have outcomes in the aggregate. Thus we shall turn to a more system-level approach, emphasizing whole electorates and examining facts through a dynamic lens. We will usually find that correct views of the facts grow stronger under information flow while misperception recedes. Many will see that as a naive proposition, but we follow the facts where they lead.

1 Perception of Facts Converges on Truth

Boulders were a problem for nineteenth-century geology. Sometimes massive and lying at seemingly impossible distances from the mountain ranges that were their origin, their placement was an explanatory problem. Far too heavy to have been moved by running water and distant from plausible streams, there was but one available explanation that fit the facts. Glaciers were known to be capable of moving heavy objects great distances.

But glaciers themselves were a problem. The distances of the boulder locations required a level of glaciation vastly greater than was known to occur on the modern Earth. Huge proportions of the continents would have to have been covered by glaciers to produce the movement. Since the size of glaciers is regulated by temperatures – expanding during unusually cold weather or contracting during warm weather – it must have been the case that there was a time – or times – in Earth's past that was quite dramatically colder than the present. Accepting the notion that there were ice ages in Earth's past broke with the naive belief that climate was constant over the eons.

But why ice ages? What was the mechanism that could alter the Earth's climate so drastically? Many were proposed: volcanic eruptions, changes in Earth's orbit around the sun, changes in ocean currents. All had some plausibility but were untestable with the primitive scientific tools of the time.

The Swedish scientist Svante Arrhenius proposed a new idea in 1896. Perhaps, he argued, the composition of gases in Earth's atmosphere was the explanation. Creating the now well-known metaphor of the greenhouse, the glass panels of which let in sunshine but retain the heat so produced, Arrhenius argued that gases in Earth's atmosphere could have the same effect. Notable changes in the composition of gases in Earth's history would explain the possibility of cycles of warmer and colder climate.

Writing when the Industrial Revolution was still relatively recent, Arrhenius even suggested that human activity – the large-scale burning of wood and coal to produce the steam power of the era – could influence the atmospheric level of carbon dioxide, a by-product. And therefore it could also produce warming. Arrhenius's contemporaries were not impressed. Human activity was considered too minuscule for global consequences. A leading counterargument seemed more plausible. Excess CO_2 in the atmosphere could not occur, it was argued, because the Earth's oceans had a near limitless capability of absorbing it.

By the late twentieth century, scientific support for the greenhouse thesis strengthened. A French and Russian team examining ice cores drilled in 1998 in

Vostok Station Antarctica found evidence of alternating cycles of global temperatures that were correlated with the levels of CO_2 and methane trapped in air bubbles in the cores. Warm periods had high levels of the gases and cold periods had low levels. Since this was hard evidence and entirely independent of the greenhouse theory, it had a powerful effect on the scientific community.

Then, as a by-product of carbon 14 dating research, the ocean absorption idea was shown to be based on a misunderstanding of ocean chemistry. It turned out that the oceans had quite limited ability to absorb excess CO_2. So the greenhouse idea gained while the dismissive ocean absorption thesis was undercut. Once thought to be far fetched, the greenhouse theory was emerging as the single most plausible account of variations in climate.

That being the case, a program of measuring atmospheric CO_2 levels was begun in the United States under the guidance of Charles Keeling. With the CO_2 and temperature relationship established, simple models began to predict future temperatures. Those led eventually to models of growing complexity that took into account complex interactions, for example, with ocean currents. By the 1980s, the forecasts began to be reliable and the message began to be disconcerting. Predictable growth in greenhouse gas levels implied future temperature increases that would fundamentally alter Earth's climate. Glaciers and polar ice packs would melt. Sea levels would rise; deserts would claim previously arable lands. See Figure 1 for a view of changing temperature and CO_2 levels.[2]

What is important to remember is that the path of climate science shifted from a large-scale skepticism of climate change hypotheses – that global climate was warming and that it was a result of human activities – to large-scale consensus. Studies of the views of climate scientists in the 1980s and 1990s put the level of consensus in the 90 percent range, and quite often as high as 97 percent. The peer-reviewed scientific literature is also nearly unanimous in support of the greenhouse hypothesis.

However, climate science shifted from an academic pursuit to one of public concern with James Hansen's testimony to the US Senate in 1981. Because human activity was implicated in the growth of greenhouse gases, human action, in the form of somehow reducing their buildup, was proposed as the remedy. Climate change now became an issue of public policy. Thus the singular dialogue of working climate scientists over theories and evidence now became two, the second a public debate about policy response.

The public debate is different – extraordinarily different. It questions not only findings and conclusions but even the motives of working scientists, whom

---

[2] Dataset accessed August 18, 2018 at https://data.giss.nasa.gov/gistemp/

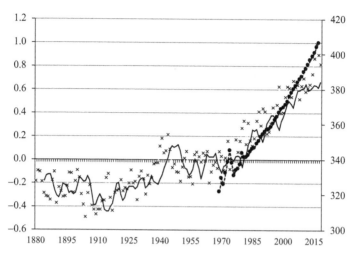

Figure 1 Global average temperatures: 1880 to 2018. Global average temperature increases on the left axis and CO_2 levels on the right axis. Data points are annual averages. The solid line is a ten-year moving average. The dotted line is atmospheric carbon dioxide level in parts per million (1969–2017).

Source: GISTEMP Team, 2018: GISS Surface Temperature Analysis (GISTEMP); NASA Goddard Institute for Space Studies

some allege to be involved in conspiracies and hoaxes. The public debate introduces forces such as political ideology and self-interest into the contest. The public is exposed to the scientific consensus but also to powerful counter-arguments that dismiss it.

The debate goes on as we write. It is far from resolved. Its ultimate conclusion, if any, will depend only partly on science. Its future course will be determined by how mass electorates respond to the flow – and counterflow – of factual evidence. That is the focus of this Element. And what can we predict of the ultimate verdict? We will see when we take up the evidence of this case – and many others – in the sections to come.

1.1 Thinking about Fact Processing by Mass Electorates

Two Questions: How Much Do We Know? and Do We Learn?

These two questions have some similarity; so it is important at the outset to distinguish between them. On the question of how much electorates know about factual issues, we concur with the scholarly consensus, not much. More carefully argued, we concur with Delli Carpini & Keeter (1996) and many others, among the most prominent, Campbell, Converse, Miller, & Stokes (1960) and Berelson, Lazarsfeld, & McPhee (1954), that citizens have quite limited interest in most public questions and that where interest is lacking, knowledge is too. We have nothing new to contribute to this conclusion.

Our focus is the related question: Do we learn? We regard most factual debates as quietly settled outside of politics. So episodes of political debate over facts are more atypical than normal. But such episodes do occur. Our focus then is dynamic, on the direction of the debate on facts over time. Our thesis, to be developed more fully in this section, is that movement over time in factual controversies is in the direction of the facts.[3] Debates do not necessarily lead to consensus, so we have nothing to say about how close or distant the public judgment is to truth, just that its net direction bends that way.

That facts matter in political debate is not a new assertion. It is a kind of folk wisdom about advertising, and persuasion in general, that claims that contain a kernel of truth are more effective than those that do not. We call this folk wisdom because it is usually assumed to be true, just itself a known fact, rather than tested. The multiple origins of this idea are evidently very old. The idea is that arguments that contain a component of known truth are therefore more persuasive than those that are pure rhetoric. Like Ronald Reagan's "Are you better off?" argument of our Preface, an appeal to an undeniable truth can be a device to convince targets of persuasion of a broader, generally less factual, conclusion.

This notion is a familiar aspect of Petrocik's (1996) party issue ownership idea. Issue ownership suggests that political parties have a history of taking one side of a policy debate and come to be recognized by supporters and opponents alike as having a historic claim to that side. In the United States, for example, Democrats created Social Security and over the decades have defended it against threats from the other side. Republicans equally are the party of tax cuts, having produced most of the biggest examples and then fended off attempts by the other side to undo them. The electorate knows these facts – and is readily reminded by political discourse.

We regularly see claims of the sort "We are better than our opponents at delivering x," a policy outcome desired by the electorate. Such claims would seem mere puffery were it not for the factual claim underlying the argument. When such claims are challenged, the challenges always provoke the best line of defense: the fact that over the decades the party has delivered x regularly – and pretty often that it has done so against the anti-x policies of the other party.

The theory of issue ownership tells us that the party that owns an issue will prevail over the opposition if a debate comes to be structured around the issue:

---

[3] For the mathematically inclined, our question is not the level of knowledge but its first derivative, the rate of learning.

who is best at delivering x? That in turn tells us that it is unwise for the non-owning party to raise such an issue.

1.2 What Factual Debates Can We Observe?

To many factual questions, there is an agreed-upon correct answer. In those numerous cases, there is no debate over a factual matter on which virtually all reasonable people agree. For something as obvious as gravity – that dropped objects do tend to fall toward the Earth – there is just no point in a debate. No one but an argumentative troublemaker will take the bait and argue against something all can see. Many, perhaps most, factual questions are in this category. We do not know enough to quantify the proportion, but surely it is very large.

Then there are things like the evolution of species, the simple question of whether or not species change over time. Nearly all credentialed scientists agree upon a correct answer, yes. And yet the Bible tells another story. So for people who believe that the sacred supersedes scientific evidence, large-scale disbelief remains. Mostly this is an issue of personal belief, and we get along fine having one dominant doctrine in secular spheres and another among some subsets of religious belief. Mostly we have no public debate on such issues. But occasionally we do. And that tells us something about why factual debates occur. Factual issues become contentious when the issue impinges on the public sphere. When we debate what should be taught to children in public schools, for example, it is not so easy to compartmentalize and let each believe what he or she wishes to believe.

More generally, we debate about factual issues when government action is involved. Smoking, for example, is usually seen as a personal choice. But secondary smoke raises collective, not individual, questions. And if public health authorities are involved, in anti-tobacco campaigns, for example, then the need to have one correct answer for all precludes simple personal choice.

A second requisite is of great practical import; we can only observe debates for which there is evidence of what the public believes. That means, in effect, that we can only study factual debates where survey organizations choose to pose questions on what the electorate believes. This is the usual issue of searching for lost keys under the street lamp rather than in the dark. It imposes an arbitrary selection on the possible topics. But there is no choice. We cannot analyze public beliefs that we do not know.

1.3 A Theory of Factual Learning

"Fact" is the central concept of this Element. Thus we begin with an all-important definition. *A fact is an empirical claim that is regarded as true by the consensus of well-informed observers*. Our usage roughly reflects the common English-language meaning of the term.

The consensus of informed observers may be wrong. So we do not make the stronger claim that a fact is absolutely true. Until the returns came in on election night in 2016, for example, Hillary Clinton was believed by the best-informed observers of politics to be the likely winner of the presidential contest. Thus the high probability of a Clinton win was a fact by our definition. Those citizens who believed that Clinton would win would be judged to be better informed than those who held the contrary view, which nonetheless turned out to be correct. After it was a fait accompli, the Trump win became a fact.

That the Earth is approximately a sphere is a fact. This is not universally believed, but people who deny it are not regarded as "well-informed observers." So, just as the consensus conclusions of science are something less than capital "T" Truth, they are a current best estimate of it. Those who dissent from scientific conclusions may be regarded either as brilliant original thinkers or merely ill taught. Most often it is the latter.[4]

1.3.1 Situating the Argument in the Literature

Americans are neither informed nor attentive when it comes to political matters (Delli Carpini & Keeter, 1996) and often they have little incentive to be (Downs, 1957). But these shortcomings are not necessarily detrimental to the democratic process (Lupia & McCubbins, 1998). Exhaustive knowledge is not a requisite for being an engaged citizen. Learning is active and goal driven; citizens will learn only as much as they need to come to reasonable decisions.

Our assertion that facts carry weight for aggregate opinion is grounded in the notion that when individual opinions are aggregated, random errors cancel out, leading to a stable and responsive public (Page & Shapiro, 1992). We join others in advocating the existence of an American electorate capable of rationally updating, where collective opinion responds to changing conditions and information in intelligible ways.

Kuklinski & Quirk (2000) observe that proponents of collective rationality confront two problems. First, errors in individual citizen's political judgments are not always random. Instead, they can be motivated. For example, partisan motivations will shape individuals' factual beliefs about the objective state of the economy (Bartels, 2002). However, as we will address in this section, these

---

[4] A note on our usage of the words "facts" and "truth": we intend to use "fact" when we are referring to observables (indicators of ultimate truth) and "truth" in theoretical and hypothetical statements. We borrow a little from the statistical convention that unknown true parameter values should be represented by Greek symbols whereas observable sample statistics are given by English letters.

motivations are not unyielding. Second, the collective opinion school has assumed that the media environment provides voters with factual information. This neglects the self-interested and manipulative rhetoric of political elites, media pundits, and interest groups that saturates political discourse. We acknowledge that deception happens, but penalties for lying and threats of verification *should* discourage elites from making false statements, at least ad infinitum (Lupia & McCubbins, 1998).

1.3.2 The Case for Motivated Reasoning

One of the most frequently cited arguments for why facts have limited leverage on public opinion is motivated reasoning, which has been consistently demonstrated to be a powerful force at the individual level. Psychological research suggests that two main drivers motivate all reasoning: (1) a desire for accuracy and (2) a desire for belief perseverance. When people engage in directional motivated reasoning, they tend to readily accept evidence that confirms their predispositions, actively argue against counter evidence, and seek out information that will support their worldview (Kunda, 1990). Thus, in an electorate where everyone engages in directional reasoning, the result is an aggregate incapacity to learn.

Directional motivated reasoning, which scholars frequently shorthand as "motivated reasoning," has been under a spotlight in recent years in both academic and nonacademic communities and has become a common explanation for recent trends linked to political polarization. This includes selective media exposure, where one avoids information that challenges prior beliefs while seeking out information that confirms them (Stroud, 2008). This also includes resistance to factual information, where sometimes factual corrections will "backfire." Evidence of a backfire or backlash effect has perhaps been most prominently demonstrated in the research of Brendan Nyhan and Jason Reifler, who in a 2010 article find that when presented with factual information about the absence of weapons of mass destruction in Iraq, conservatives became *more* certain that they had been found.[5] However, comprehensive replication studies have since found little evidence of a backfire effect, suggesting that it is in fact quite rare (Coppock, 2016; Guess & Coppock, 2018; Wood & Porter, 2019).

Despite contemporary political polarization, we remind readers that motivated reasoning, while seemingly ubiquitous, does not always occur. Yes, it can

---

[5] A large body of scholarship also examines the consequences of providing factual information on policy attitudes and preferences (Berinsky, 2007; Gaines, Kuklinski, Quirk, Peyton, & Verkuilen, 2007; Hopkins, Sides, & Citrin, 2019) that we do not engage with here. In this Element, we do not make claims for how factual information and beliefs shape subjective opinions. Our question is more limited: Do factual beliefs converge toward truth?

likely shape issue opinions for the politically sophisticated, those who are passionate and knowledgeable about certain issues (Taber & Lodge, 2006). But partisan motivation declines among ambivalent individuals, who have little interest or concern with political debates (Druckman, 2012; Lavine, Johnston, & Steenbergen, 2012). Such weakly opinionated, ambivalent individuals constitute a substantial portion of the American public.

But for those who are susceptible to directional motivated reasoning when processing facts, what motivates them to learn? Experimental research suggests that people will begin to rationally update their beliefs under the right conditions. Redlawsk, Civettini, & Emmerson (2010) find that in the face of repeated disconfirming information, there is an "affective tipping point" at which individuals ultimately "stop reinforcing their preferences, abandon motivated reasoning, and begin rational updating" (p. 564). When confronted with factual information consistently and repeatedly, we are more likely to learn. We expect this pattern of rational updating to carry outside of experimental settings. Citizens are exposed to copious amounts of competing signals daily. But when consistently confronted with the facts, we expect them to ignore the noise and update their factual beliefs in the accurate direction.

Overall, the case that is often made for motivated reasoning neglects several factors that are of importance if we are to understand the role of facts in public debates. First, scholars seldom consider the role of the larger information environment on opinion (for notable exceptions, see Jerit and Barabas [2006, 2012]). Individuals can only process the information that is available to them in their environment; therefore, considering the information signals citizens receive is important. Second, attitudes toward issues are not static; they can evolve and be shaped by the volume and content of information encountered over time. To determine if facts have significant leverage in political debates, it is important to examine how the public responds across time as those facts are likely to become more apparent. Finally, scholars of American politics often direct their attention to those who embrace falsehoods and not the bigger picture: the electorate as a whole. We turn here to thinking about how the flow of factual information is processed.

1.3.3 Models of Fact Acquisition

Imagine fact acquisition as a sequence. We are each bombarded by a flow of factual claims over time. We ask questions like "Is x true?" and receive for answers the sequence of claims. The question then becomes "How do we process the sequence?" There are three possibilities, two of them not very realistic. One possibility, call it *One Shot*, is that we take the latest datum in the sequence as true, ignoring everything that came before. Another, call it *Cumulative*, is that we cumulate all the information we have received and take a mental average to come to a net conclusion. And the last, call it *Dynamic*, is that we form a conclusion on each occasion – which becomes weightier as more information contributes – and update that conclusion by weighing the previous conclusion against the new claim.

One Shot

The One Shot model has the citizen making a new conclusion entirely from the most recently encountered fact. Its advantage over the other two is simplicity. Its disadvantages are two. It produces changing, and therefore inconsistent, conclusions. Second, it is radically inefficient for producing quality conclusions. The valuable information of a lifetime of observations is ignored. Perhaps citizens function this way when they care so little that they have no utility for correct beliefs. But if they care at all, the inefficiency is an intolerable cost.

Cumulative

In the Cumulative model, the citizen observes all the signals that say x is true or x is not true and comes to believe in the dominant proportion of signals. Since the clarity and credibility of signals will vary, the judgment about proportions will be more complicated than a simple average. This model uses all the available information and so improves on the One Shot model. Its defect is that it takes no account of the decay of human memory processes. Recent information, that is, is more vivid and available than is old information. See Zaller (1992) and Zaller & Feldman (1992) on this point. So it is quite unrealistic to assume, as this model must, that a fact learned twenty or thirty years ago will carry the same weight as one learned today.

Dynamic

The Dynamic model, which also goes by the name Bayesian Updating, is highly familiar in the literature on decision -making (Gerber & Green, 1998). In it the citizen encounters a new fact in the sequence and asks him- or herself whether an existing belief is in need of revisiting. If so, the citizen does not treat the new fact as deciding – as in the One Shot model – but instead as one more piece of information in a sequence. The prior belief, because it is likely to be based on a lifetime of experience, will generally weigh more than the new fact. But if the new fact agrees with prior belief, the prior belief will be strengthened. If it disagrees, the prior belief will be weakened.

The term "Bayesian Updating" and its mathematical underpinning come from Bayes' Rule, a formalization of rational decision making. It is a guide to optimal decision making about perceived truth in light of both prior belief and new information.

Because there is scientific skepticism about citizen rationality and about the ability of ordinary people to manage probabilistic information, Bayesian Updating is often considered an ideal of rational processing more than a theory of how human decision makers actually cope. We will argue that the skepticism is overblown.

In the notation of Hill (2017), S is a signal that a statement is true or not true and T and F are the states true and false respectively and Pr is probability, Bayes' Rule is as follows:

$$Pr(T|S) = Pr(T) \frac{Pr(S|T)}{PR(S|T)Pr(T) + Pr(S|F)Pr(F)} \qquad (1.1)$$

If one can recover quantitative values for each of the terms in the rule, one can, in principle, compute the exact probability with which a subject believes a statement to be true, given the prior belief and the signals about it that he or she has received.

In observational research, it is never the case that exact values for all of the terms of the rule are known. Thus one can never know the degree to which the rule is predictive of actual human behavior. Hill's (2017) elegant experimental design overcomes this problem. Although the experimental situation might be far removed from the messy business of assessing contested facts from sources of varied credibility, its beauty is that the rule can be exactly quantified. As Hill's findings are central to our claim of how individuals function in processing a stream of information, we deal with the design and outcome of the study at length.[6]

1.3.4 Hill's Experiments on Bayesian Updating

Hill begins with an online subject pool weighted to represent the population proportions of a Pew mass survey. Subjects in the experiment rate six political evaluative statements as true or false. One of the six, for example, is the true statement: "From 2009, when President Obama took office, to 2012, median household income adjusted for inflation in the United States fell by more than

---

[6] We focus on Hill's work for detail and clarity. For other experimental research demonstrating that citizens learn in a way that is consistent with Bayes' Rule, see Coppock (2016) and Guess & Coppock (2018).

4 percent." As would be expected from theories of confirmation bias and motivated reasoning, Republicans are modestly more likely to rate the unfavorable statistic as true of the Democratic president.

Then each of the subjects is exposed to four signals, saying that the statement is true or not true. Subjects are told (accurately) that the signals are correct three times out of four on average. Subjects rate the truth of the statement after each signal. Bayes' Rule permits the calculation of the exact probabilities – and hence sample proportions – with which the statement would be rated true if the subjects were updating perfectly according to Bayes. After all four signals are received, the actual proportions rating the statement true can be compared to the proportion based on pure Bayesian Updating.

The observed result for the example case is an initial rating of truth (the prior) of 57.8 percent of the sample and a final rating (the posterior) of 73.5 percent. That is, subjects on average move in the direction of the truth. The partisan subgroups do the same. Democratic subjects have a prior of 49.9 percent and move to a posterior of 74.4 percent. Republicans have a prior of 63.0 percent and a posterior of 73.8 percent. Although their initial ratings differ, both move toward the truth as they receive more information.

Hill makes three observations from the data for the six statements:

1. Participants learn. Their posterior beliefs are closer to the truth in most cases than their prior beliefs.
2. Participants do show partisan motivation effects of the expected kind.
3. While there is partisan bias, there is no partisan polarization. Democratic and Republican beliefs always move in the same correct direction in response to the signals.

Participants, however, are not perfect Bayesians, as all would expect of a mass sample. A regression analysis shows that subjects update, on average, 73 percent as much after four signals as would be predicted for perfect Bayesians. They move toward the truth, that is, but not as much or as quickly as would a perfect updater. In terms of statistical significance, it can be said that subjects do learn; the percentages rating the statements correctly are significantly higher for the posterior than for the prior. But also they are significantly imperfect; the actual posterior is significantly less correct than the Bayesian perfect standard. Hence Hill's main title, "Learning Together Slowly."

We conclude with Hill that Bayesian Updating is a viable model of citizen fact processing, but that ordinary people are impaired Bayesians, processing more slowly than the Bayesian ideal. That conclusion has two fundamental parts: (1) citizens do move toward the truth as they process factual information flow and (2) they do not do so as rapidly and efficiently as the Bayesian ideal. The latter part is clearly what would be expected of citizens who are tuned out of the factual information flow and put a low utility on getting the answer right.

From Micro to Macro

Thus we have a picture of an individual citizen who encounters signals about the truth of factual controversies and tends, slower than optimally, to correct his or her beliefs in the direction of the facts. But our question is of the electorate, the aggregate of all citizens. If our micro model of (slow) Bayesian Updating holds for individuals, what then can we infer for aggregates? What follows is our fundamental thesis, that over time mass electorates' beliefs about facts tend to converge on truth. Because our micro information processor is suboptimal we cannot say anything about how quickly or slowly convergence is expected. But we can say that given enough time, mass beliefs about facts will tend to correct.

1.4 Why Convergence on Truth?

Why does the truth carry any weight to us? What does it matter whether or not our perceptions are accurate? Learning has been a critical tool for human survival. If one sees a venomous snake on the ground, it can be fatal to believe it is harmless. The same is the case if one believes smoking tobacco is good for the lungs. Oftentimes the stakes are not quite so high. But historically, it pays to learn.

Our definition of "fact" is consensus on the truth of x by well-informed observers. Therefore it follows that to the degree that consensus exists, citizens will tend to encounter uniform, not conflicting, signals. The weight of those uniform signals will move prior beliefs steadily in the direction of truth.

We expect convergence on facts to manifest in one of two ways. For facts that are static, say former President Barack Obama's place of birth, we should see the public converge toward this fact over time. These facts never change. Obama was born in Hawaii, and this will not change next year or the year after that. But the factual evidence and attention given to that evidence over time provide repeating signals that a growing portion of the public should come to receive and accept.

The second case involves facts that in themselves are dynamic. These factual realities are always in flux: inflation, unemployment, crime. They are moving targets, and we expect the public to move in the appropriate direction of the target, on average. Most likely the public cannot estimate real conditions with precise numerical accuracy. However, we expect that it is tuned into the ebbs and flows of the facts, which can only be captured with a dynamic perspective.

Belief in facts is not infinitely malleable. When people are feeling prosperous, you cannot convince them that they should be depressed. When depressed, messages of good cheer fall flat.[7]

But it is not always the case that citizens encounter a single consensual source of factual information. Sometimes facts are contested in public debate. We can imagine two alternative scenarios. (1) Sometimes the signal of true facts comes surrounded by the noise of unsystematically wrong alternatives. These randomly wrong counter-assertions will slow the learning process. But because randomness is self-canceling under aggregation, convergence on facts will still occur. It is just slowed.

But what if there is a source of information that is systematically wrong? This is Scenario 2. And in partisan or interest-dominated environments, it will occur with some frequency. If there are two sides to a debate, there will often be a party or industry group that chooses to assert the opposite of the truth. In this scenario, the citizen is exposed to systematic falsehood – and perhaps equally often as the truth. Then our convergence result does not occur.

1.4.1 A Marketplace of Ideas: A Note on Information Flow

A central component to our thesis is the notion that collective opinion will follow information flow. But in a state with freedom of speech and of the press, information flow is never uniform. When truth is contested and relevant to the public sphere, a public debate emerges. What follows is a dance of information signals: truth and untruth continue to compete until one has prevailed. This is the core concept behind "the marketplace of ideas" metaphor, originally put forth by John Milton in 1644, who famously writes "Let her and Falsehood grapple; who ever knew Truth put to the worse, in a free and open encounter?" This line of thinking was used to justify the need for freedom of speech, as it would always lead to truth, the optimal outcome. Stanley Ingber observes the implications of the model by positing that "the market model avoids this danger of officially sanctioned 'truth'; it permits, however, the converse danger of the spread of false doctrine by allowing expression of potential falsities. Citizens must be capable of making determinations that are both sophisticated and intricately rational if they are to separate truth from falsehood" (Ingber, 1984, p. 7).

The marketplace today looks far different from what it looked like in 1644. Indeed, it looks quite different from a few decades ago. Technological advancements have provided us with more sources of information to choose from than ever. Such a media environment allows us to live in echo chambers, where we can choose to expose ourselves only to ideas that fit our worldview. The

---

[7] We borrow this point from previous work (Stimson, 2015).

consequence is that there is little competition between ideas when there is no exchange of them.

Many of today's media sources have a detectable partisan bias, but several engage in outright inaccurate and false reporting. This is the case for a number of right-wing fringe independent media sources, such as the websites Breitbart or Gateway Pundit, as well as a few liberal-leaning sites, such as Occupy Democrats, that do not have the journalistic standards that established media outlets have (Faris et al., 2017).

This is where the importance of a marketplace comes in. Yes, the reach and prominence of radical online platforms that spread conspiracy theories and hoaxes are alarming. But fake news consumption is heavily concentrated among a *small* minority of Americans (Guess, Nyhan, & Reifler, 2018). So, indeed, there are Americans who fit the narrative described in Scenario 2: they are repeatedly exposed to consistently systematic falsehoods. But we conjecture that truth will prevail not through a single mind but through the collective. So what do we make of modern America's "marketplace of ideas"? It is admittedly imperfect, but not necessarily defunct.

Ultimately the marketplace of ideas model suggests that truth will prevail. In the following section, we conjecture about why truth has this leverage.

1.5 Evidence and Inference

The fundamental assertion of this Element is that public views on factual questions tend to converge toward truth over time. But, like all scholars, we do not get to observe "truth" itself. Instead we must content ourselves with "facts," the consensus beliefs of informed observers of a question. The evidence that we can observe is whether mass publics move toward the dominant information flow about facts. From that observation, we wish to infer movement toward truth.

The history of science underscores the slippage between the two concepts, facts and truth. The consensus of informed observers is not guaranteed to be true. But neither is it the case that observable facts are unconnected with truth, if it could be known. People and organizations that comment on facts, science, government, scholarship in general, and journalism at its best have incentives to produce true statements about the world. It would produce laughter if a college physics class taught that the Earth is flat, for example. So norms about truthfulness may be hard to observe, but they are powerful.

Information flow, that which ordinary citizens observe, is not guaranteed to be truthful. But neither is its average truth value neutral. Truth struggles with untruths to dominate. Sometimes those untruths are relatively random mistakes; in this case, we expect the mixture of the two, truths and mistakes, to aggregate toward relative truths. The one is systematic and strengthened under aggregation. The random component tends to cancel out.

But there are also motivated falsehoods, often produced by people and organizations that have a stake in the issue. In the climate change example, organizations that benefit from producing greenhouse gases wish to argue, in various forms, that the greenhouse theory of climate change is wrong. And motivated falsehoods are not at all random. Just like true beliefs, they are strengthened under aggregation. So if there are competing versions of the facts, there is no guarantee that truth will outweigh falsehood. In the pages to come, we will observe instances in which false claims appear to have dominated the information flow to which citizens are exposed.

So what do we assert about observable facts and unobservable truths? We assert that (1) truth is uncertain and (2) it is advantaged. The second of these claims needs explication. In many aspects of life, there is an incentive to be right. Polling firms, for example, profit from having the reputation of being right. They could tweak their results to aid one side or the other. But to have a future in which they sell their product on a competitive open market, the reputation for accuracy is almost priceless. Imagine a debate between competing parties about who will win an election. The claims of the two would tend to be offsetting. But enter in a third component, polling results, and now the aggregate mix of information is *on net* in the direction of the polling results. Truth is uncertain, but it is advantaged.

Smoking, we believe, really does have numerous negative impacts on health. Smokers will encounter a debate, "smoking is safe" vs. "smoking is dangerous." And then they will encounter a view from a credible neutral source, such as their own personal physician, that smoking is dangerous. And the mix will tilt toward the truth. So again, the truth is advantaged.

The climate change debate is two sided, with loud voices on each side, "climate change is happening" vs. "climate change is a hoax perpetrated by scientists trying to profit from their views." Between the two, either could dominate. But now consider that working climate scientists are continuing to do research and report on it, so the consensus view of climate science is added to the information flow. That tilts the mix toward the position that climate change is happening. So, overall, there are situations in public discourse where it is reasonable to expect an advantage on the side of truth.

1.5.1 Pathologies

Recall our Scenario 2 described earlier, where information flow is tainted by systematic falsehoods. We can imagine an extreme form of Scenario 2 where the false signal actually dominates public discussion. Here our prediction is that public belief converges on falsehood. This is a pathology. It is a case we should not expect to witness often, but we cannot rule it out as a possibility.

Where party debates about facts exist, citizens exposed to partisan argument will tend to converge on the party consensus, which may not be true. Consider an example. In 1999, when asked what would happen to Social Security if no changes were made within the next twenty years, about 34 percent of Americans said it would completely run out of money.[8] Six years later, a survey by CBS News and the *New York Times* found that a whopping 63 percent of respondents expressed the view that the Social Security system would "be bankrupt by the year 2042 if no major changes are made." This statement is definitionally false because bankruptcy protection is for individuals and businesses, not governments. Social Security has a $3 trillion trust fund, where annual income exceeds benefit payouts and thus the fund grows each year.[9] So why did so many Americans continue to believe that Social Security is insolvent?

This case illustrates two conditions that contribute to, and are probably necessary for, systematically false beliefs. One is the existence of a systematic campaign of false information. That exists. Social Security is one of the most popular programs of all times. That leaves few options open to opponents of the program. If current recipients and those nearing retirement age cannot be persuaded to oppose monthly benefits, the age group open to persuasion is people too young to see retirement in their near future. And the argument that works for them is to claim that the system they are paying taxes to support will no longer exist when they reach retirement age. And thus that false message is heard with great regularity in public debate on the airwaves. A related line of attack is that the trust fund is not real, just an "IOU" it is sometimes claimed. Its backing, in fact – the very same as the backing of the US dollar – is "the full faith and credit of the United States."

A second condition, certainly in this case and perhaps more generally, is that there is a kernel of truth in the false claim of bankruptcy. The system does face a demographic threat to future stability. The retirement of the baby boom generation will create a condition in which annual payout will eventually exceed annual income. That is why a trust fund exists. That will probably require adjustments at some future time to either increase revenue or decrease

---

[8] Survey by Americans Discuss Social Security. May 3–May 17, 1999.

[9] This growth will not continue much longer as payout levels are rising to meet income levels and will eventually exceed them. When that occurs, the fund will begin to be reduced annually. In the hypothetical possibility of going to zero, the current income is about 79 percent of expected future payouts and thus the program could continue indefinitely at 79 percent of current benefits – or at current or increased benefit levels with a tax increase.

benefits. So that *is* a problem, even if calling it bankruptcy is a false characterization. We will see other pathological cases in the sections to come.

The Illusion of Controversy

By now many readers must be thinking that we are naive, taking a rose-colored glasses view of a world of facts riddled on every side by falsehood. If we look at all the current controversies – those that provoke survey organizations to pose questions – in every case we find people asserting falsehoods. But to understand this we need to ask what happens to factual controversies as they approach consensus on the truth. The answer is that such questions stop being posed in surveys. We do not ask people if they believe the sun will rise tomorrow or that dropped objects fall to Earth. In politics, we ask who will win an election before election day. We do not ask who has won after election day. Such questions produce uninteresting data in which everyone gives the same response. The cases we see are those in which large numbers of respondents assert both sides. When "issues" are no longer "controversies," they cease to be suitable questions to pose. So the only questions posed are ones in which numbers of respondents assert falsehoods.

1.6 A Post-Truth Society?

The 2016 presidential election brought us the term "fake news." Its aftermath in the presidency of Donald Trump has often been called a post-truth society. There is some accuracy in this characterization. Keeping track of the president's false and misleading statements has become something of a national pastime. An Element about facts can hardly ignore the widespread spouting of falsehoods, "alternative facts" in the phrase of a presidential spokesperson.

Certainly some things have changed in American society. Citizens once got their news from organizations that cherished a reputation for telling the truth. Journalism is a human endeavor and therefore imperfect. If journalists did not always get the facts right, we can at least say that they tried. That cannot be said of social media or the internet that makes them possible. We have always had the spread of accounts, many false, by informal means, rumors. But social media give rumors a megaphone. Falsehoods can now be shouted to the whole world – and then reposted.

But we should be wary of any account that asserts a fundamental change in human behavior. We humans perhaps owe our ability to screen truth from falsehood to our evolutionary heritage. Those ancestors who saw threats and opportunities in nature accurately were more likely to survive and reproduce than those who got it wrong. Such a long-developed aptitude does not change with a presidential election or a president. Such trendy descriptors as "post-truth" may accurately characterize the zigs and zags of cultural change that characterize a period. They do not characterize a new state of human behavior. The same old rules keep shaping behavior.

1.7 The Evidence of Trends

In the analyses to come, we often display evidence of changing public views over time. The question will arise: Are these true trends or merely chance variations that look like trends? This question is answered with statistical tests for linear trend. We have performed these tests with the result that all but a couple such learning series trend significantly ($p<.05$). We do not present the tests but will note the exceptions.

The literature on policy preferences often posits aggregate cycling behavior. The stimulus is cycling of party control. The response is relative movement away from the party in power as a rational response for moderates who find both parties' positions excessive. We do not expect cycling behavior here. Who controls government and what they happen to believe should have no impact on what individuals believe. Perhaps a warm connection to a regime should make individuals more likely to believe what the regime asserts to be true. But that should be offset by an opposite movement of those who dislike the regime, becoming more likely to disbelieve. On net we expect no cycling.

1.8 Organization of the Element

At a time when commentators are impressed by the power of "fake news" and scholars increasingly focus on false beliefs in the mass public, we assert an old, underappreciated, truth: facts matter. In this Element, we do not present a single way in which to test our predictions. We must rely on public opinion data where similar questions have been asked consistently over time. Thus, to determine if there is a tendency to converge on truth, we look at a wide variety of cases, most of which support our expectations. Some pieces of evidence we bring to bear are heavily inspired by prior scholarship; we integrate them with new evidence to create a fuller picture of the leverage facts have on macro opinion.

Each section in this volume takes on a different factual theme. In Section 2, we turn our attention to economic facts. Similar to Reagan's "Are you better off?" we illustrate how the public perceives economic conditions over time. Though Americans rely on a partisan lens when evaluating the economy – more positively when the president is of the same party and vice versa – by and large aggregate perceptions follow the highs and lows of true conditions. Evaluations are not scattered or misinformed like some pundits might lead us to believe.

They are organized and predictable, following economic realities with surprising accuracy.

Section 3 focuses on explicitly political facts. This includes perceptions of the outcome of presidential elections both before and after elections have been held. We also provide several historical case studies of factual controversies that have directly implicated American presidents, including Watergate, weapons of mass destruction (WMDs) in Iraq, and President Barack Obama's place of birth. Together, we observe a tendency for public opinion to converge on the facts, even amid contentious partisanship and misinformation. With each case study, we illustrate over time public opinion on the facts and speculate as to the conditions that led to opinion change.

Section 4 illustrates public opinion on a collection of factual debates that have been frequently politicized. This includes a discussion of how Americans have come to learn about topics related to science, including tobacco's health risks, evolution, vaccination safety, and climate change. We also include a discussion of moving target facts, including economic inequality and crime. We bring these varied cases together with the hopes of illuminating when opinion converges on facts and offer some conjectures as to why. To conclude Section 4, we discuss pathological cases that do not support our thesis. We end this Element with a brief conclusion in Section 5, summarizing our main arguments.

2 Economic Facts

Imagine that you have randomly selected a group of ordinary Americans from all walks of life and you pose to them a simple question, "How would you rate the condition of the national economy these days? Is it very good, fairly good, fairly bad, or very bad?"[10] and collect the responses, the numbers who chose each of the four options from "very good" to "very bad." Then you repeat the same procedure with a different randomly selected group every month for a period of decades. You graph the net rating, using say the percentage of all respondents each month who chose one of the two "good" categories, "very good" or "fairly good."

What do you have? At one level you have just an ordinary graph, showing ups and downs over time. At another level what you have is astonishing. Because these crude judgments by ordinary people – probably not an economist in the bunch – look just like the summary judgments of professional economists. The two lines plotted in the same graph are hard to tell apart. And they are closely associated with standard measures of the real economy, as we will see in this section.

These ordinary people who produce the ups and downs of the graph are real-life Democrats and Republicans who see the economy through a partisan lens.

---

[10] This is the CBS News/*New York Times* version of the question.

Given the bias that we reasonably expect from that, how could the net result be accurate? And yet we have known that it is for decades.

These sorts of economic evaluations have posed a problem for political science because they do not fit our prevailing view that the mass electorate is uninformed. We examine this exceptional case in this section. In the end, we will come to doubt that it is all that exceptional.

2.1 A Moving Target

The state of the economy is a moving target. There is no answer such as good, bad, or in between that is correct for all time. It is constantly changing. A correct assessment of last month may be incorrect this month.

With a moving target, we cannot simply assert that perceptions converge on facts because what were facts in the recent past may no longer be facts after the convergence process has run its course. Instead we require a dynamic conception. The conception that works is that disequilibrium gets corrected – assessments that are too high or too low move toward just right over time. That implies error correction – that whatever the direction of error in assessment at the current time, it will move in the opposite direction at the next time.

That will be our prediction, that when assessments are on net too high or too low, they tend to correct themselves at the next time period. An electorate that learns from information flow will tend to move its assessments in the same direction as the real economy. One that does not will repeatedly err in the same direction, without any correction process.

2.1.1 Partisan Bias in Perceptions

Citizen perceptions might always be in error from simple ignorance. However, with the state of the national economy a second problem – partisan bias – arises. The two facts almost universally known by the American public are the identity of the president of the United States and the political party he (or one day she) represents. Given that fact and the widely held view that presidents are responsible for the state of the national economy, it is quickly apparent that partisans are likely to misperceive the economy as better than it is – when they share the president's partisanship – or the opposite – if they do not.

The theory of motivated reasoning is the most plausible challenge to an assertion of accurate learning of facts, economic or otherwise. It posits that humans see the world with two goals: accuracy and consistency. The accuracy goal is from our evolutionary heritage. Accurate perceptions increased the probabilities of survival and reproduction. Consistency is driven by the need for cognitive balance, to see the world without the stress of entertaining contradictory beliefs. The story then is that the two goals compete in daily behavior so that perception is a mix of the two. We wish to see the world accurately, but only insofar as those perceptions do not result in stress.

The theory then predicts that perception will be accurate, but within the limits of keeping our mental house in order. That, in turn, means that we tend to see that which is consistent with what we already believe, a bias toward confirmation. Add partisan bias to the picture, the idea that we wish to see results that support a preexisting affective commitment to one side or the other of the party debate, and we have a basis for expecting false perceptions.

So which is it, accuracy or partisan bias? It would seem at first glance that it cannot be both. Either people see the performance of the national economy for what it is or they see a distortion that reifies their prior beliefs in the competence of their own party and its opponent. But could it be both? Could partisans closely track the real economy *and* see it through the prism of distortion? That is the question to be answered in the analysis that follows.

2.2 Do Partisans See the Same Economy?

The question, as always, for motivated reasoning is how much perception is driven by the accuracy motivation (predicting partisan agreement on the facts of the economy) and how much is driven by the consistency motivation (predicting perceptions biased by which party controls the White House). In this section, we draw heavily on the work of Evan Parker-Stephen, published Parker-Stephen (2013) and unpublished Parker-Stephen (2007).

For a first look at accuracy and consistency, we array perceptions over time and by party identification groupings. See Table 1. We look first at the entire time period of available data and then at the fifteen-year span, 1986–2000. The later period is chosen to show patterns before a high level of party polarization became evident.

What emerges are impressive levels of agreement on the facts of the economy in the early period of the presidencies of Ronald Reagan through Bill Clinton followed by much greater divergence of evaluations of the state of the economy in the Bush (43) through Obama years, 2001 to 2015.[11]

Our expectation of the role of motivated reasoning in this case is that the party of the White House and its partisans in the electorate should rate the economy as better than it actually is. The "in" party gets credit for success and blame for hard times. So its partisans should see things as better than they are on the party's watch. The party out of the White House is the reverse. It is likely to emphasize evidence of failure and minimize evidence of success. So we need to

---

[11] The data were no longer collected after 2015.

Table 1 Correlations of Ratings of the US Economy by Party
Identification Groups, 1986–2015

| | Entire Period: 1986–2015 | | |
	Republicans	Independents	Democrats
Republicans	1.000	0.868	0.460
Independents		1.000	0.822
Democrats			1.000
N = 297			

| | 1986 to 2000 Only | | |
	Republicans	Independents	Democrats
Republicans	1.000	0.949	0.861
Independents	1.000	0.963	
Democrats	1.000		
N = 107			

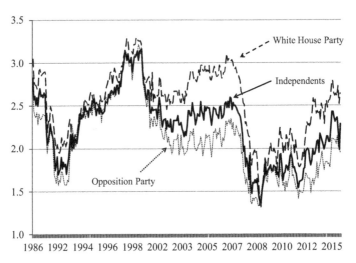

Figure 2 Ratings of the US economy by party identification groups, in party, out
party, and independents, 1986–2015

Note: Higher values on y-axis indicate more positive evaluations of the economy.

structure our graphic look at the data by classifying partisans as "in" party, "out"
party, and independent. We present that look in Figure 2.[12]

---

[12] Most of our data series in this Element comes from irregular surveys spanning several (or several
dozen) years. Our x-axes are designed to best illustrate when surveys were taken.

Table 2 Decomposing bias and accuracy: Percentage of in party, out party, and all respondents who see the current economy as very good or somewhat good

Party Group	Percentage Very Good or Somewhat Good	Party Bias
In Party	59	12
All Respondents	47	
Out Party"	35	−12

Note: Average ratings over 297 CBS/*New York Times* surveys, 1986 to 2015.

Here we see a clear manifestation of directional motivated reasoning. The in party nearly always rates the economy as better than the outs or independents and the "out" party nearly always rates it as worse than the other two. The gap between in and out evaluations is often quite large, particularly in the polarization period, 2001–2015. In the pre-polarization period the three lines are tightly clustered together and the net positivity sometimes deviates from the motivated reasoning expectation.

As Parker-Stephen noted in his earlier analysis, this is not a question of whether ratings of the economy impress by their net accuracy or by their partisan bias. Both are true. They *are* biased by partisanship – strikingly in some cases – and they *are* accurate on average. See the summary in Table 2, where both patterns are evident. Partisans are biased – a nicely symmetric twelve-point bias by both in and out parties on a simple scale of percentage of "good" ratings. The in party respondents see the national economy as about twelve points better than the consensus rating of all respondents and the out party sees it as twelve points worse.

2.3 Does the Public Track the Facts of the Real Economy?

We have seen a relatively high level of agreement on the state of the national economy. But we also need to know whether it is the actual economy reflected in consensus ratings or some kind of illusion, a perceived economy quite different from reality. Perhaps the media conspire to paint a picture of economic facts that is systematically different from reality. Our skepticism of media coverage and strong partisan feeling about media bias would be consistent with such a story.

So how then can we tell if subjective ratings match real facts on the ground? Again following Parker-Stephen's lead (Parker-Stephen, 2013), we emulate the real economy by predicting the CBS/*New York Times* ratings from four real

Table 3 Regression predicting CBS/*New York Times* consumer sentiment from four economic indicators

	Coefficient	Standard Error	t	p
Unemployment	−0.164	0.008	−19.87	0.000
Inflation	−0.056	0.009	−6.17	0.000
Disposable Income	−0.002	0.008	−0.23	0.820
Gross Domestic Product	0.072	0.007	9.90	0.000
Intercept	3.303	0.073	45.51	0.000

N = 297
Adjusted R^2 = .75

measures of economic performance: (1) the unemployment rate, (2) the inflation rate, (3) annual percentage changes in real disposable income, and (4) annual percentage growth rates of (real) gross domestic product.

The point of the exercise is to see if subjective ratings of economic performance closely approximate the facts of real performance indicators. See the regression in Table 3. There we observe that three of the four indicators strongly predict the subjective evaluations.[13] The fit, R^2 = .75, tells us that most of what survey respondents see when they rate the economy is based on economic facts.

But we can go further. The regression of Table 3 allows us to create a prediction of what consumer ratings should be if only the four indicators of the regression drove ratings. Call this prediction "emulated ratings." Emulated ratings, a linear combination of the four indicators, convey the facts of the real economy without any subjectivity or misperception. The emulated series is our best approximation of what a fully objective judge would conclude by considering only the facts of the four indicators. It is a summary of hard facts, not subject to any of the ills of human perception. Figure 3 graphs the survey respondent summary ratings (labeled "Perceived") alongside the emulated series, predicted by the four indicators (labeled "Actual"). One can see what we knew from the statistical fit, that the two track closely together.

With the emulated series in hand to estimate the hard facts of the economy, we can now compare these hard facts to what potentially biased partisans claim to be the facts. Figure 4 is similar to Figure 2 except that we replace the independents' rating of the economy with our estimated factual economy.

---

[13] The fourth, real disposable income, is a strong predictor in a bivariate analysis but is so highly correlated with the GDP measure of growth – with which it is definitionally almost interchangeable – that it loses its explanatory power in a fully specified model.

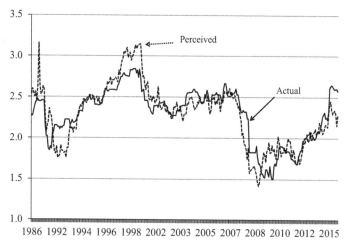

Figure 3 CBS/*New York Times* consumer sentiment, actual and predicted by four-indicator regression, 1986–2015

Note: Higher values on y-axis indicate more positive evaluations of the economy.

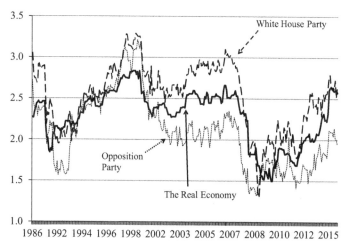

Figure 4 Ratings of the US economy by party identification groups, in party, out party, and predicted real economy, 1986–2015

Note: Higher values on y-axis indicate more positive evaluations of the economy.

Here at last we confront the puzzle that motivates this analysis: "How can it be the case that partisans accurately perceive the national economy if their ratings are strongly influenced by partisan bias?"

The picture shows visually what statistical measures of correlation tell us in a more spare fashion. Despite very large biases driven by partisan misperception (documented in Table 2), both the White House partisans ($r = .89$) and their opposition ($r = .79$) closely follow the tracks of the real economy. And if that is true, it must also be the case that they closely follow each other! And they do ($r = .80$).

Since the party groups are of similar size and the two biases are of similar magnitude, the positive bias of the in party and the negative bias of the out party offset each other producing an aggregate signal that closely tracks the real economy. If we were to ask how accurate were the individual judgments of survey respondents, the answer is "not very." At the individual level, the partisan bias impresses more than the factual accuracy. But if we pose the same question for the aggregate electorate, accuracy impresses while the self-canceling bias is hidden.[14]

In Conclusion

We started our examination of perception of facts by choosing the case that was known to produce impressive evidence of factual cognition. As we turn now to political facts, and in Section 4 to facts about issues and policies, we will see similar evidence. Lacking the excellent measurement of the economics realm, these other kinds of facts will largely support the same thesis.

What about the future? The correlations of Table 1 and the visual evidence of Figure 2 jointly tell a story. They show that partisan bias was smaller and overall accuracy of perceptions greater in the recent past than both are today. They show that the partisan polarization of the current era has diminished the accuracy of economic – and probably other – perceptions. We have no basis to project even greater polarization into the future or, equally, to expect the current high level to dissipate. But the trend is not encouraging.

3 Facts about Politics

In 2016, motivated by a turbulent presidential election in the United States and the controversial "Brexit" referendum that shook the world, Oxford Dictionaries named the term "post-truth" as the "word of the year." News organizations now hire journalists whose job is exclusively to fact-check the claims made by political elites. This attention to fact-checking has been invigorated by the political success of Donald Trump, who by May 2019 totaled at least 10,000 publicly stated falsehoods. [15] Though Trump is an extreme

---

[14] Again we note that there is little novelty in this analysis. The design and fundamental conclusions are borrowed from Parker-Stephen's unpublished original work. Although we have modestly extended the time span of the analysis, our analytic design closely follows the original.

[15] Glenn Kessler, Salvador Rizzo, and Meg Kelly, *The Washington Post* (April 29, 2019).

example, he was by far not the first to introduce factual uncertainty to our political discourse. To better understand how the public today comes to see the facts, in this section we examine a series of events and issues that have been central to American politics. When we look at these cases from a dynamic perspective, we find a tendency for opinion to converge toward facts.

3.1 Presidential Races: Who Will Win?

Beneath the contest for votes in a presidential election is a second contest, for expectations. Both probable winners and probable losers have a motivation to shape voter expectations of the outcome. The probable winner needs to maintain emotional tension about the race, lest supporters take the outcome for granted and stop putting forth effort. The probable loser needs to maintain an image of viability to motivate his or her base. It is OK to be merely behind. But if voters conclude that a race is hopeless, that is a self-fulfilling prophecy.

So there is always a partisan contest over voter expectations. And thus motivated reasoning comes into play. Both sides are expected to succumb to the message of their own side. But the daily news also bombards individual citizens with the facts of the matter, for example, horse race polls. We are told with some frequency who is ahead and who is behind and by how much. We can choose not to believe, that polls are not reliable, that they are "skewed" for some nefarious purpose. But if candidate x leads candidate y day after day after day, before long it becomes very hard to resist the message that x is ahead. We expect citizens to resist messages they don't like, but when the facts are repeated over and over we expect resistance to fade.

But what are the facts? What is a reasonable and objective expectation of the outcome of an election? Voters are exposed to numerous polls, forecasts based on objective factors, forecasts based on polls, and punditry based on whatever particular pundits attend to. There is both consensus and conflict in this information flow. For a single best summary of this information flow, we choose a "betting" market, a daily summary of the beliefs of well-informed people putting their own money at risk. The presumed motive of market investors is to make money by being right. At least we are willing to assume that that is the case.

We put the matter to a test in an analysis of the presidential elections from 1988 to 2016, the period for which the Iowa Electronic Market (IEM) data are available. Looking at the *net* perceptions of the race by the whole electorate – Democrats, Independents, and Republicans – we seek to ask who wins in the contest between partisan spin and the facts of the betting market information. For each survey in which respondents are asked to say who will win, we have the previous day's closing price of the IEM winner-take-all market for the Democrat to win.

The facts voters are exposed to are the various objective forecasts, such as those by the *New York Times* and *Five ThirtyEight* and prediction or betting markets. Any of these would do, but we choose the Iowa Electronic Market winner-take-all market for its longer availability. We assume that voters who do not consult such sources will see their message reflected in public commentary on the election by those who do.

The question is: "Do voters follow the flow of factual information about the expected outcome or do they resist,?" perhaps to insist that their own favorite party or candidate is winning? We measure citizen expectations with survey questions such as the CBS variant, "Regardless of how you intend to vote for President in 2016, who do you expect to finally win the 2016 presidential election – Hillary Clinton or Donald Trump?"

In Figure 5 we display what survey respondents predicted by the value of the IEM winner-take-all market for the previous day, in both cases using the two-party share for the Democratic candidate for president. We assume that the electronic market tracks closely with the best-informed observers of politics and summarizes the flavor of the election news voters were exposed to.[16]

What is readily seen in Figure 5 is that respondent answers to the who will win question are strongly associated to the price of shares in the Iowa market.

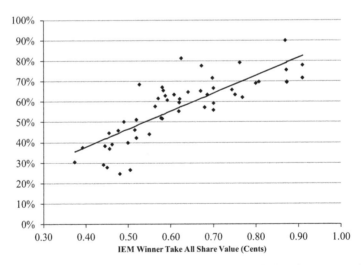

Figure 5 Who will win the presidential election? Predicting the Democratic candidate will win the presidential election from the Iowa Electronic Markets winner-take-all share price, in cents: 1988 to 2016 (scatter plot with regression line).

---

[16] We do not assume that voters pay attention to this or other prediction markets. That is not necessary. Those who prognosticate on the airwaves do.

Table 4 Proportion expecting the Democratic candidate to win the current presidential election predicted by Iowa Electronic Markets "Democrat to win" share value, 1988 to 2016 standard

Variable	Coefficient	Error	t
Democrat Share Price	87.518	8.633	10.14
Intercept	2.824	5.479	0.52
N	55		
Adj. R^2	0.653		

What ordinary people say in surveys, that is, is closely associated with what investors putting their own money at risk believe about the election outcome.

A more formal test is given by the regression that produced the straight line in Figure 5. We put the matter to a test in Table 5 where we predict the proportion saying that the Democratic candidate is the likely winner[17] from the IEM winner-take-all share price for a Democrat to win.[18] The t value more than 10 is strong evidence of the bivariate connection where some 65 percent of the variance is accounted for.

There are two issues with the data in Figure 5 and Table 4 that are potentially troublesome. One is that the data are a mixture across the eight presidential elections, 1988 to 2016. It might be the case that most of the association is due to between-election differences, that some are one sided and easy to call. Perhaps it could be argued that voters get it right in one-sided contests but are little better than guessing for close contests. It should be noted that this set of eight elections includes no landslides such as the earlier 1964, 1972, and 1984 contests.

The other issue is that data availability is uneven across elections. Surveys are numerous for the most recent contests, 2008, 2012, and 2016, but sparse for the earlier contests. So our conclusion that voters closely track publicly available information about elections might be mainly true for the recent contests.

To deal with these two problems, we break out the most recent contest, that of 2016 between Hillary Clinton and Donald Trump, for individual analysis. This

---

[17] The actual questions give candidate names, not parties.

[18] The winner-take-all market pays $1 after the election for each share of the eventual winner and nothing for the loser. So this market rewards the investor who calls the winner correctly. This is comparable to the question facing survey respondents, "Who will win?" The alternative, "vote share" market has a payout value determined by the vote share. It rewards getting the size of victory or defeat correct.

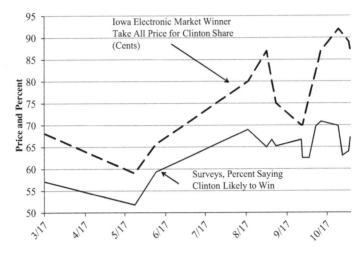

Figure 6 Sixteen surveys tracking the expected winner (percentage) of the 2016 presidential election contest against same-day values of the Iowa Electronic Markets winner-take-all share value for Democrats to win (price, in cents)

election, so close that most observers called the outcome wrong, clearly does not benefit from mixing close with one-sided elections. There is no mixing, by design, and a contest in which the popular vote winner lost the election that mattered is as close as it comes.

We have data at sixteen points in time, from March to November 2016, about voter perceptions of who would win the contest, Hillary Clinton or Donald Trump. And we have data about elite expectations as well, for which we again utilize the Iowa Electronic Market winner-take-all share prices, an instrument for examining how the politically active and involved betting their own money on the outcome saw the race shaping up.

The ups and downs of the 2016 contest can be seen in Figure 6. Note in the figure that while citizens are not as confident of a Clinton win as market participants (by about 10 points), the mass sample's perception data do nicely track the betting market data as a signal of the likely election outcome ($r = .72$). Undoubtedly the aggregate data cover up some motivated reasoning going on among individual citizens. But the message of the facts comes through clearly. The explained variation for this one case is less (.49) than we saw when we mixed elections (.66), but in this close contest ordinary people's views of the outcome were still strongly similar to those of the informed market participants.

3.2 Presidential Races: Who Has Won?

We have seen that in the aggregate, Americans can predict the outcomes of presidential elections with striking similarity to the predictions used by election experts. We now turn to a much simpler and more straightforward question concerning high-profile elections: "Who *won*?"

Of all the facts we discuss in this Element, who has won a presidential election is among the most obvious. So obvious that seldom have pollsters opted to ask respondents about it. Yet, there have been times in American history when the winner has been called into question. In uncertain cases such as these, pollsters turn to the court of public opinion.

The public's perceptions of electoral outcomes are best illustrated by two recent presidential elections in particular: George W. Bush versus Al Gore in 2000, and Donald Trump versus Hilary Clinton in 2016. Both these highly contentious elections resulted in the Electoral College favoring the Republican candidate, whereas the popular vote went to the Democratic ticket. The two elections differed widely in the source of uncertainty; though for both, election day was followed by a barrage of contestation, confusion, and competing information signals.

3.2.1 Bush vs. Gore

Commenting on the 2000 presidential election, comedian Argus Hamilton remarked, "At the rate we're going, the Inaugural Ball is going to be a surprise party." The days and weeks following November 7, 2000, were by all accounts a mess.

On the evening of the election, a clear winner failed to emerge. The news media reported sometimes contradictory conclusions from exit polls, due to a handful of narrow state races. Initial election returns indicated Gore had won the popular vote (by more than half a million votes), but whether Bush or Gore won the number of electoral votes required to win the presidency was undetermined.

It all came down to Florida. Media outlets prematurely declared Gore the winner based on state exit polls, but Bush emerged to be in the lead once actual votes from Florida were tallied. However, Bush won by so narrow a margin that Florida state law mandated a machine recount. Gore's campaign made a request for ballots in several counties to be manually recounted, a request that was granted by a state court. Bush appealed the decision, and the case made its way to the US Supreme Court. A series of legal battles lasted several weeks. The Supreme Court decision in *Bush* v. *Gore* was announced on December 9 and ordered the manual recount to be halted. Florida's electoral votes were awarded to Bush, winning him the presidency.

The election riveted the nation. By December 2000, more than 91 percent of Americans said they were following the results of the election *very or somewhat closely.*[19] Americans were paying attention. Through repeated media attention to the event, it became further and further apparent that though the Electoral College was still undetermined, Gore indisputably won the popular vote.

American voters had never seen such a contested presidential election. A candidate had not won the Electoral College without winning the popular vote in more than a century. Pollsters never asked citizens who won the presidential race overall, but they did ask who received the popular vote. The percentage of Americans reporting Gore had won the popular vote is illustrated in Figure 7. From November to January, the percentage of Americans reporting Gore had won the popular vote rose from 64 percent to 78 percent, while the percentage of the public believing Bush did nearly cut in half (from 24 percent to 13 percent). Despite the dispute over the recount in Florida, the facts had increasing leverage. Citizens slowly moved toward accepting the truth: Gore had won more individual votes than Bush.

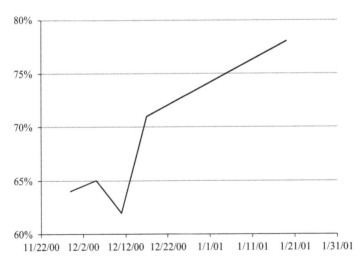

Figure 7 Percentage of Americans reporting that Al Gore won the 2000 national popular vote

Source: CBS News Poll

---

[19] Survey conducted by CBS News, December 9–December 10, 2000.

3.2.2 Trump vs. Clinton

Several electoral cycles later, the United States faced a similar situation yet again. In contrast to the numerous polls, forecasts, and betting markets that all anticipated a Clinton victory, on November 8, 2016, Americans elected Donald Trump as president. This time, however, the Republican candidate garnered a strong Electoral College victory with 304 electoral votes to Clinton's 227. Clinton, on the other hand, received nearly 3 million more individual votes than her opponent.

The election outcome did not go without its fair share of controversey. Similar to the polemic campaign that preceded it, the results were the focus of extensive scrutiny and attention. In the months following Trump's victory, the extent of Russia's meddling in the election to undermine Clinton would be made public. The election results were also disputed in relation to concerns over voter fraud, voter identification laws, and voter disenfranchisement.

Reactions from more than one side sought to delegitimize the results. Notably, weeks after the election Trump tweeted (inaccurately) that he would have "won the popular vote if you deduct the millions of people who voted illegally." Green Party candidate Jill Stein also raised questions over the veracity of the election results by raising millions of dollars to hold recounts in several states.

But again we ask: What are the facts? Determining what the outcome of the election would be without Russian interference, or with different state voting laws, is difficult. We can speculate, but we can never observe the counterfactual.

However, the facts can tell us who won the election and by how much. So again, amid controversy, we wanted to see if Americans could tell us who won. Unfortunately, with only two national surveys asking this question, there is not a surplus of evidence to go on. By the end of November 2016, 66 percent of Americans reported Clinton had won the popular vote.[20] Approximately a week later, Pew Research Center found that 72 percent of Americans reported Clinton winning the popular vote, whereas 78 percent reported that Trump had won the most Electoral College votes.[21]

In an era of deeply partisan news and echo chambers, one might expect the electorate to be more evenly split on who won the presidency than in years past. But public opinion on this topic in 2016 looks quite similar to that in 2000,

---

[20] Survey conducted by Gallup, November 28–November 29, 2016.
[21] Survey by Pew Research Center, November 30–December 5, 2016.

where on average three out of four Americans were able to accurately identify the winner of the popular vote and the Electoral College. Again, amid controversy and a flood of competing signals, the facts had leverage.

3.3 Facts in the Face of Political Controversy

Controversial issues of right and wrong have always colored our politics. Often these issues, while having some factual basis, are controversies of ideology and preferences. We choose to look at politicized issues that were exclusively about the facts – where there is a definitive right and wrong answer. In this section, we discuss some of the most covered and contentious factual controversies in American politics in the past several decades: Richard Nixon's involvement in the Watergate scandal, weapons of mass destruction (WMDs) in Iraq, and Barack Obama's birthplace. They are also fruitful for our purposes as they have been a repeated topic of discussion for polling houses.

3.3.1 Watergate

"What did the President know and when did he know it?" That famous question, posed by Senator Howard Baker (R., Tennessee), focused the attention of senators, members of the House, and millions of others in the United States and almost everywhere abroad. There is the question, unresolved to this day, of whether Richard Nixon ordered the Watergate break-in that unleashed the Watergate scandal and destroyed the Nixon presidency.[22] But the Baker question was about another fact, did Nixon know about the cover-up of the Watergate incident? And on that question we eventually learned the truth. He did.

John Dean, counsel to the president, testified to the Senate Watergate Committee – and to a worldwide live audience – that Richard Nixon was the mastermind of the cover-up scheme. And that testimony was subsequently bolstered by the "smoking gun" tape of Nixon, six days after the failed break-in, instructing H. R. Haldeman, chief of staff, to order the Central Intelligence Agency (CIA) to tell Federal Bureau of Investigation (FBI) leaders not to investigate the case because the break-in was a CIA operation.

---

[22] Another fact, similarly unresolved, is the answer to the question "Why?" What did whoever ordered the break-in expect to learn by tapping the phone of Lawrence O'Brien, chairman of the Democratic National Committee? What could have been learned that was so important that it would justify the obvious risk of the break-in? Speculation has it that it was something to do with O'Brien's relationship to the billionaire Howard Hughes, who was also a Nixon donor.

What was the factual status of the matter of Nixon's involvement in a cover-up? The answer to this question depends upon the information flow. In the first eight months of the story, there was no Watergate scandal. There was merely the curious story of the failed break-in. Although some leads existed that would in time reach Nixon's door, the story was barely kept alive in the pages of *The Washington Post* ; in most media outlets – print and electronic – it did not exist at all. Connecting this "third-rate burglary" to the Nixon White House was just too farfetched, even among the many Nixon foes. Admittedly, this was hard to believe after what we learned later. But for evidence of the lack of a scandal, one need look no further than Nixon's historic reelection victory margin five months after the break-in. Survey organizations did not probe public response to the scandal because it was not yet a scandal.

Beginning in early 1973 facts about a possible cover-up of the break-in began to emerge. FBI Acting Director L. Patrick Gray testified in January that John Dean, White House counsel, had probably lied to the FBI about Watergate. Then on March 17 James McCord, one of those arrested for the crime, shocked the world with a letter to the presiding judge, John Sirica, that asserted that the trial had been tainted by perjured testimony and that a high-level cover-up was ongoing. When that letter was read in open court, the curious incident of the break-in at the Watergate office complex became the Watergate Scandal, as explosive as it had earlier been quiet. This led to the May Senate Watergate hearings, firings of White House senior staff members, and eventually to John Dean's testimony that Richard Nixon had personally directed the continuing cover-up of the Watergate affair.

In this second phase of the story, there was an abundance of factual information. But there was also a counter flow. Nixon's partisans defended his actions. While it was hard to deny some kind of cover-up, it was plausible to assert that it was the doing of White House underlings, with the president putting a stop to it as soon as he was informed. So there were two plausible stories emerging: "Nixon guilty" and "Nixon not guilty." And naturally, party ties would affect which of the two people believed.

As the subpoenaed Nixon tapes began to be released, they showed that John Dean's testimony was correct, virtually word for word, undermining Nixon's defense. The "smoking gun" tape ended this second phase. When that evidence became public, Nixon's defenders one by one gave up the defense and announced that they too would vote to impeach. The tape release ended the counterargument. Although it lasted only a few days, this third phase of the Watergate story featured rare unanimity on the facts. Nixon was guilty.

The data: beginning in early 1973, survey organizations began to query the American public on various attitudes toward Watergate. Much of the result is unhelpful because of constantly changing context – and therefore constantly changing survey questions. But on one issue, whether Richard Nixon was aware of a cover-up of the affair, there are similar questions asked over about an eighteen-month span. While the questions are not identical, the issue itself totally dominated the news for this period, perhaps to a degree that no other issue has attained. So we think that differences in question wording should have little effect. These are very strong attitudes, pro and con, not the weakly held stances that characterize typical policy preferences.

We have no data for the initial period, when the issue was underground. For the second period, when information flow was abundant but partisan, we are unsure what to expect. And we have a single survey, in the field after the release of the smoking gun tape, where we expect convergence on the now uniform truth of Nixon's involvement. We present the data, the percentage saying that Nixon was aware of the cover-up in Figure 8.

What should we expect of the public opinion? First we consider the second period, after Dean's testimony implicating the president and before the release of the smoking gun tape in late July 1974. The news was all bad for Nixon. The

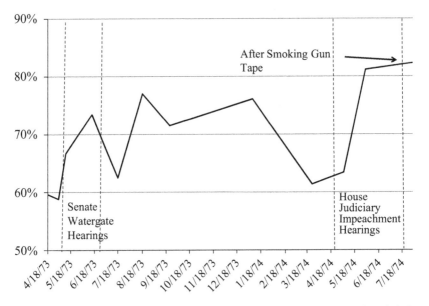

Figure 8 Was Richard Nixon aware of a cover-up of the Watergate break-in?
(1973–1974)

Note: Responses were re-coded into either "aware of the cover-up" or "not aware of the cover-up." "Don't know" responses are dropped from analysis.

Source: Roper Center for Public Opinion Research

actual break-in was a crime for which all of those caught in the deed either pled guilty or were convicted. And that the crime had been covered up was not in doubt. The options came down to two. Nixon had either (1) recruited a collection of criminals for the White House staff who operated a cover-up without his knowledge or (2) he was in on it. Because of the dominantly negative news flow, we expect gradual convergence on the truth of Nixon's involvement. And then a single survey exists after the release of the tapes when all the news implicated Nixon himself in the cover-up. There we expect convergence on truth.

All of the data of Figure 8 are from surveys taken after John Dean testified that Richard Nixon masterminded the Watergate cover-up. So it is clear that opinion had shifted dramatically since the 1972 Nixon reelection triumph. If we had data before the break-in was tied to the Nixon White House, the public did not yet know of a cover-up, let alone its link to Nixon. After the testimony, never fewer than about 60 percent of Americans expressed the belief that Nixon was implicated in covering up the crime. After an amazing sequence of events, the appointment of a special prosecutor, the disclosure of taped conversations, the "Saturday Night Massacre" (firing of prosecutor Archibald Cox), and the *U.S.* v. *Nixon* Supreme Court decision, that percentage drifted (unevenly) into the 75 percent–80 percent range. It reached about 80 percent in the last available survey, just after the tapes were released. It would have risen higher still if Nixon had not terminated the controversy by resigning.

3.3.2 Iraq and Weapons of Mass Destruction

In October 2002, President George W. Bush went on record saying that the Iraqi regime had "a massive stockpile of biological weapons that has never been accounted for and is capable of killing millions." The notion that Iraq possessed weapons of mass destruction (WMDs) was one of the motivating forces behind the US invasion of Iraq in March 2003. This statement was consistently communicated to the American people by both President Bush and members of his administration and was frequently pointed to as the rationale for the invasion. Indeed, at one point Bush proclaimed to the nation there was "no doubt that the Iraq regime continues to possess and conceal some of the most lethal weapons ever devised." Eventually the Bush administration's doubtless "facts" were revealed to be inaccurate.

United Nations searchers were unable to locate any such stockpiles.[23] Doubts were then seeded by David A. Kay, lead researcher in the Iraq Survey Group,

---

[23] Bush administration figures publicly questioned the competence of the UN search. But it was later learned that the locations the UN team was searching had been provided by the US Central Intelligence Agency.

a large-scale investigation by the Pentagon and CIA to search for the alleged stockpiles. In October 2003, Kay suggested "we were all wrong, probably" about whether Iraq had stockpiles of nuclear, chemical, or biological weapons. In 2004, the Duelfer Report was released, and it confirmed earlier suggestions that the scale of weapons the Bush administration described was inaccurate. Small-scale chemical WMDs were found, but the quantity was not sufficient to pose a significant threat. Ultimately, there was no evidence that Iraq had begun any large-scale program for weapons production by the time of the American invasion. The Duelfer Report suggested that though Iraqi leaders had the desire for such weapons, they did not have the capacity. Iraq did have chemical weapons at one point, but these were destroyed during Saddam Hussein's rule. Following the Duelfer Report, the Bush administration accepted the fact that WMDs were nonexistent in Iraq and ceased its search for them. In the years that followed, it was repeatedly confirmed to the public that Iraq did not have an active WMD program.

It is important to note the Bush administration was not the only source culpable of exaggerating the presence of WMDs without reliable intelligence. Some national media sources were at fault as well. One example that made headlines was the case of Judy Miller, the national security reporter for the *New York Times*. Miller wrote numerous articles about Iraq's weapons program that were informed by unreliable or dubious sources, allowing the reputable publication to contribute to the false narrative of WMDs in Iraq.

Overall, this is what we know. The American public was given information that Iraq possessed WMDs, and that information was untrue and unverifiable at the time. Some researchers examining opinion on this issue have asked whether voters believed that Bush intentionally misled voters (Hochschild & Einstein, 2015). Such questions, though, tap opinions that are not fully grounded in facts. They are speculative. We cannot, for example, fully know George W. Bush's state of mind about the weapons claim. But we are able to know whether or not the United States *found* WMDs in Iraq.

When turning to public opinion, we focus exclusively on what is known. Figure 9 shows the percentage of the public that said that WMDs had been found in Iraq between 2003 and 2011. Overall, we see a steady decline in the percentage of Americans who asserted that WMDs were found. It reaches its lowest point, 16 percent, at the end of the series. (The trend of this short series is in the right direction but does not attain statistical significance.) As the Iraq war dragged on, it became unpopular, as wars typically do. But part of this decline in popularity is due to the fact that one of the main objectives of the invasion was unattainable because it was based on false pretenses. So as the war became more unpopular, we suspect that this went hand in hand with more Americans coming

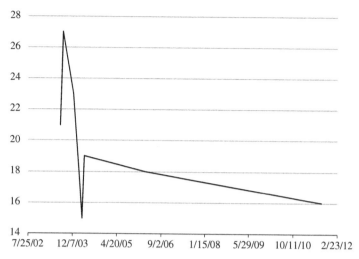

Figure 9 Percentage of Americans who say the United States did find weapons of mass destruction in Iraq (2003–2011)

Note: "Don't know" responses are dropped from analysis.

Source: Roper Center for Public Opinion Research

to terms with the fact that large stockpiles of nuclear, chemical, and biological weapons were not being found.

What was found, at various times, were remnants of an earlier stockpile of chemical artillery shells left over from the Iran-Iraq war of 1980 to 1988 that were corroded and leaking gas. That the American forces suffered fourteen gas exposure injuries just from the act of disposing of them suggests that they were no longer in usable condition. However, the fact of the matter is that tools for mass destruction were not to be found in Iraq.

3.3.3 Barack Obama's Birthplace

A final case of factual controversy that became divisive on partisan lines were questions of Barack Obama's religion and place of birth. The rumor that Obama was not born in the United States, what now we often describe as "birtherism," can be traced as far back as 2004, when Illinois political candidate Andy Martin suggested that Obama was a Muslim and had lied to the American people about where he was from. Birtherism received widespread attention when Obama ran for the 2008 Democratic presidential nomination, with Martin filing a lawsuit against the state of Hawaii to release his birth certificate. The circulating rumors were at times erratic and multi-faceted – suggesting he was born in Kenya or in Indonesia, conflating religion and birthplaces. However, they all served the purpose of pushing the narrative that Obama was un-American. The rumor gained steam during the 2008 Democratic primary, even being propagated by some Clinton supporters. Speculation that Obama was not born in the United States followed him as he continued into the general election, and soon his campaign released a copy of his short-form birth certificate.

By November 2008, nine out of ten Americans reported either hearing or reading about Obama being a Muslim and six out of ten had heard or read that Obama did not qualify as a US "natural-born" citizen (Garrett, 2011).[24] The rumor was fueled by partisan divisions, in addition to anti-black and ethnocentric sentiments among whites (Pasek, Stark, Krosnick, Tompson, & Payne, 2014). Though the birther conspiracy was mainly cultivated by some fringe right-wing media, it reentered public consciousness in 2011 when then–TV personality Donald Trump demanded that Obama release a long-form birth certificate. The pot was being stirred yet again, and the Obama administration released his long-form birth certificate the following month.

The controversy over Obama's birthplace was ignited and fueled by attacks from political opponents. Following the release of both his short- and long-form birth certificates, the facts were clear. Trump did not admit to the facts until September 2016, as the Republican nominee for president. After much pressure, Trump finally conceded, saying "President Barack Obama was born in the United States. Period."

The percentage of Americans reporting that they believed Obama was born somewhere outside of the United States is shown in Figure 10. The graph paints an interesting picture in that through the height of the debate – specifically, throughout most of Obama's tenure in office – 20 percent to 30 percent of Americans reported that Barack Obama was born outside of the United States. However, following the release of his long-form birth certificate in 2011, this number declined until it hit its lowest point, 11 percent, in 2018. Although the overall trend line is significantly downward, the movement is far from uniform, with the first three years showing movement away from the facts.

What can account for this shift? We expect that when the quality of evidence is high (i.e., a publicly released birth certificate), partisans who may have normally jumped at the opportunity to endorse the rumor as an opportunity to partisan cheerlead lost the motivation to do so. When the evidence is undeniable, some people should reach a tipping point, where accuracy motivations overcome partisan motivations. We also observe that fewer Americans come to

---

[24] Even if the birtherism rumor of foreign birth had been true, Obama would still have been "natural born" under prevailing constitutional interpretation because his mother was an American citizen at his birth. Ted Cruz, a 2016 candidate, had a similar claim, birth in Canada to one parent who was an American citizen.

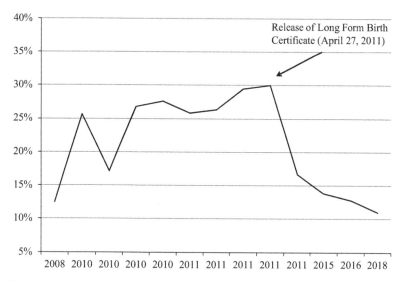

Figure 10 Percentage saying that Barack Obama was not born in the United States (2008–2018)

Note: Responses were re-coded into either "born in the US" or "not born in the US." "Don't know" responses are dropped from analysis.

Source: Roper Center for Public Opinion Research

report Obama was not born in the United States *after* his presidential term had ended. This also speaks to the role of motivation: one reason people report a belief in falsehoods is an effort to express their partisanship. By saying that Obama was not born in the United States, one might be insinuating his or her opposition to his presidency. But when the candidate is no longer the president, the incentive to endorse a known falsehood declines.

4 Facts about Issues and Policies

We now turn to facts that extend beyond the scope of politics and elections, and look to specific issues. How does the American public do when faced with questions of science, or when asked to assess real-world trends?

We illustrate aggregate opinion over time on several salient issues, some more relevant today than others. We offer insight into these issues and speculate as to why the mass public moved toward the facts for some and not for others. A limitation to our method of case selection is that we did not have much method at all. With no way to randomly sample factual issues, and with limited time series data, we chose the cases in this section for data availability. Particularly, we looked at several cases for which we have a substantial time series for survey items that tap factual perceptions. We keep this selection limitation in mind in our conclusions. However, we hope that by examining a range of topics and issues, we might develop a deeper understanding of when and why aggregate opinion converges on facts.

4.1 Questions of Science

Debate over science-based facts is ubiquitous today. Do early childhood vaccinations for certain diseases cause autism? Are genetically modified foods unsafe for human consumption? Was HIV purposefully spread by the federal government? These public debates all engage in some degree of conspiratorial thinking, which pundits and scholars alike argue has gained steam in recent decades. This supposed rise in conspiratorial thinking has been attributed to shifts in technological developments, particularly the Internet, that have transformed how we produce, spread, and consume information (Barkun, 2013).

With all of the attention that is given conspiracy theories and their proponents in recent years, we were curious to know how some of the oldest and most notorious falsehoods are perceived by Americans. Consider one of the earliest revolutionary scientific discoveries: the Earth is round. At one point in time, respected scientists believed the Earth was flat. Yet when presented with solid evidence indicating otherwise, the scientific community eventually changed its stance, supporting the facts. Though the planet's shape was established as fact centuries ago, conspiratorial thinking on this subject lingers. But just how pervasive is this thinking? In 2018, 2 percent of Americans reported firmly believing the Earth was flat.[25] Of course, if Americans always got the facts right, this number would be zero. But it is not far from it.

Two percent is not quite as threatening as some news headlines would lead us to believe: in 2017 the *Economist* published an article entitled "America's flat-Earth movement appears to be growing" and in 2018 the website *Vox* ran a how-to article entitled "How to argue with flat-earthers." This media coverage hones in on real-life flat-Earth conspirators, describing their large following on popular sites like YouTube and Reddit, and their attempts to organize and influence others. But the reporting of flat-Earth conspirators' can inflate our perception of how rampant this belief is. Survey data tell a simple story. Americans have overwhelmingly accepted a long-established fact.

Scientific findings that have been less established, on the other hand, may be more prone to doubt and debate. In the following sections, we explore some recent scientific debates, where the facts clearly come to reward one side.

---

[25] YouGov poll, April 2, 2018.

4.1.1 Tobacco

In 2015, when asked if smoking tobacco had negative health consequences, 98 percent of Americans said yes. The strength of this consensus is rarely found in the history of public opinion polling. Though acknowledging the link between smoking and various forms of diseases is commonplace today, for a large part of the twentieth century this was not the case. Tobacco advertisers not only used lifestyle and value-oriented advertisements to target consumers; they also frequently made factual appeals as well. Consider the advertisement by Lucky Strike from the early 1930s seen in Figure 11. In large letters the advertisement reads, "Face the facts!", making implicit claims that smoking is innocuous to one's health ("This is non-irritating!").[26] For tobacco companies to be successful, they could not just appeal to Americans' desire to be slim and cool. They had to appeal to people's grasp of reality too. Advertisers knew that facts (or perceptions of facts) mattered. A similar ad used medical journals for a scientific-sounding claim: "When smokers changed to Phillip Morris, substantially every case of irritation to nose or throat – due to smoking – either cleared up completely or definitely improved. According to a leading medical journal."

Figure 12 illustrates that since the 1950s, Americans have evolved to conclude – with a drastic turnaround – that smoking had negative health consequences. In 1954, fewer than 60 percent of Americans reported that tobacco affected health, and this number climbed 38 points by 2015. But to what can we attribute this drastic shift? In the mid-twentieth century, the number of scientific studies documenting the tragic effects of tobacco on public health was multiplying. In 1964, the US Surgeon General's report *Smoking and Health, Report of the Advisory Committee to the Surgeon General of the Public Health Service*, officially recognized the serious health risks of tobacco, representing the first large-scale effort by government to address the risks of tobacco. In the following years, Congress passed a series of laws requiring tobacco companies to include warning labels on their products.

Public and private efforts to warn the public about the harms of tobacco were met with widespread misinformation campaigns targeting consumers. And the influence of industry money and lobbying in Washington was impressive. At the outset of the political contest over tobacco use, the tobacco industry was certain that people's weaknesses for its products would prevail, and consumer interest would be protected by elected officials (Derthick, 2012). People wanted to

---

[26] The claim in smaller print: Lucky Strike, the finest Cigarette you ever smoked – the Cream of the Crop – "IT'S TOASTED." Lucky Strike has an extra, secret heating process. Everyone knows that heat purifies and so 20,679 physicians say that Luckies are less irritating to your throat.

Figure 11 Smoking leads to good health: An Early 1930s Lucky Strike
advertisement

smoke, and government would do what the people wanted. The industry proved
to be more wrong on both counts than one would have guessed. Eventually the
correct consensus among the public emerged, despite large misinformation
campaigns by powerful corporations. But why did the facts prevail?

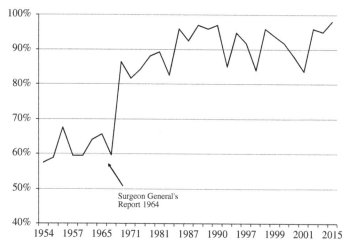

Figure 12 Percentage of Americans who say smoking tobacco is causally related to cancer (1954–2015)

Note: "Don't know" responses are dropped from analysis.

Source: Roper Center for Public Opinion Research

We have a couple of explanations. First, government is uniquely equipped to spread information. Before any government intervention, anti-smoking efforts were led principally by nonprofit organizations such as the American Cancer Society and the American Lung Association, which had a fraction of the resources of government.

The federal government would eventually make strong efforts to spread the fact that those who smoke cigarettes are much more likely to develop – and die from – certain diseases than people who do not smoke. For example, in 1966 the United States became the first country in the world to require health warning labels on cigarettes. Then, later in 1967, the US Fairness Doctrine required public service announcements about smoking's health risks to counter tobacco ads on radio and TV. Government was motivated to spread factual information, and it did so fervently.

Government did not just have the ability to spread factual information on the health risks of tobacco; it also actively worked against those spreading misinformation. In 1970, Congress passed the Public Health Cigarette Smoking Act, which banned cigarette ads on TV and radio and strengthened the surgeon general's warning label on cigarette packs. The last televised cigarette ad in US history aired in 1971, during *The Tonight Show starring Johnny Carson*. In the late 1990s, the Department of Justice filed a lawsuit against major tobacco companies for deceiving Americans about the health hazards of smoking. All of this is to say: government had important leverage on what information flowed to Americans.

Our second explanation why public opinion over time moved toward the facts is the nature of the fact itself. It is personally relevant to people in ways that many facts discussed in public discourse are not. The cost of rejecting the warning that smoking cigarettes is deadly, or even that secondhand smoke has negative effects on health, is high. To believe that tobacco is non-hazardous makes one more likely to engage in behavior such as smoking, putting oneself personally at risk.

Over the past few decades, we have seen a notable convergence toward the facts in terms of the risks of tobacco. What's more, this shift in opinion has had behavioral consequences: fifty years after the first surgeon general's report on smoking, 18 percent of American adults report smoking, compared to 42 percent in 1964.[27] However, it is important to note that acceptance of the facts did not lead to an equal acceptance on what to do about it. Though many Americans came to accept that smoking was hazardous, some were reluctant to support big government's meddling. For example, in 1995 Congress member Mike Synar (D., Oklahoma) told a conference of anti-tobacco activists that they had "confused the public's support on the facts with their lack of support on the values." But our question is not what do people do with the facts they have, but do mass electorates converge toward the facts or away from them. Ultimately, when information is readily available, clear, and relevant, they move toward the facts.

4.1.2 Vaccines and Autism

One of the more recent factual controversies affecting public health involves early childhood vaccinations and autism. The debate began in 1998 when British researchers published a paper stating that the measles-mumps-rubella (MMR) vaccine caused autism. The study drew criticism for its methods and the publication was ultimately retracted by the journal. Since then, at least a dozen studies have been conducted, each of which has found no evidence that vaccines cause autism. A 2004 review by the Institute of Medicine asserted that "the evidence favors rejection of a causal relationship between thimerosal containing vaccines and autism." The scientific consensus is clear. However, the 1998 study received substantial publicity since its publication, which grew

---

[27] Of course, the anti-tobacco campaign has not been purely fact based. Various anti-smoking campaigns have included emotionally evocative rhetoric, graphic images, and appeals to citizens' emotions that have promoted learning about the health risks of smoking (Durkin, 2012).

exponentially when Hollywood celebrities drew attention to the study. This issue was hot.

Given the publicity around the controversy, and the high-profile status of those who doubted the scientific community's consensus, what did the public think? A March 2015 Gallup Poll asked respondents "Do you personally think certain vaccines do – or do not – cause autism in children, or are you unsure?" Only 41 percent of the sample said no. However, a whopping 52 percent reported being unsure. Fast forward to spring of 2018, when a Fairleigh Dickinson University Poll asked Americans if it has been proven that childhood vaccines cause autism.

This time, 72 percent of respondents said vaccinations did not cause autism, and only 10 percent said they were unsure. In three years, we saw a whopping thirty-point shift in public opinion in the direction of the facts. But why?

We entertain a couple of possibilties. First, we expect that public interest in the debate fluctuated over time; after that interest subsided, more members of the public were likely to end up on the side of the facts. To illustrate variations in interest over time, we used a simple key word search trend on Google, shown in Figure 13, which displays search interest of the words "vaccination" and "autism" together. Interest in the topic in the United States skyrocketed in

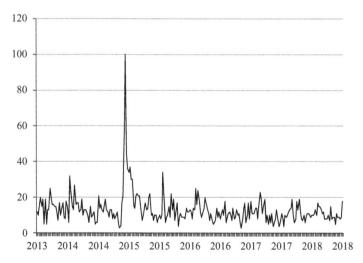

Figure 13 The Incidence of "vaccination" and "autism" Google searches, weekly, (2013–2018)

Note: Numbers represent search interest relative to the highest point on the chart. A value of 100 is the peak popularity for the term. A value of 50 means that the term is half as popular.

February and March 2015, and then drastically dissipated. We expect that at the height of a factual controversy, people had a variety of competing considerations, leading to mixed positions. But eventually the clouds cleared, and the facts showed through. The public followed.

Second, we expect that similar to the case of tobacco, government has a capacity to dismiss rampant falsehoods, particularly ones that pose a threat to public health. A study published in 2018 in the journal *PLOS Medicine* argued that the growing anti-vaxx movement led to an increase in measles outbreaks in the United States, leading to the first death due to measles in a *decade* (Olive, Hotez, Damania, & Nolan, 2018). This was the result of a rising number of personal belief exemptions (PBEs), based on religious or philosophical beliefs that parents were obtaining to opt out of having to vaccinate their children. The study connects the declining number of vaccinated children with campaigns that warned of the risks of vaccines. This phenomenon is particularly prevalent in metro areas such as Portland, Oregon, and Austin, Texas, cities that are highly populated by white liberals, who are more likely to believe vaccinations are unsafe (Hochschild & Einstein, 2015a).

Growing numbers of PBEs have led to increases in disease outbreaks across the country. In this case, factual misperceptions have had serious, life-threatening consequences. But similar to the case of tobacco, the federal and state governments have the authority to effectively intervene. One method is passing laws that establish the real risks of not vaccinating children. California, a state that saw a huge rise in PBEs between 2000 and 2015, notably passed a law in 2015 that banned many of these exemptions parents were using. The new law effectively increased the statewide immunization numbers. Similar to laws that prohibit smoking in public spaces, the California state law communicated the fact that certain behaviors were health risks to others.

We expect that government policy could lead to a shift of opinion on vaccinations similar to what we saw in Americans' views of tobacco. Time will tell, but initial government efforts, combined with news of disease outbreaks, may have already motivated opinion to shift. A poll conducted by University of Michigan's C. S. Mott Children's Hospital found that in 2015, more than a quarter of parents were more likely to believe vaccines were safer for children than a year prior. As Jeffrey Kluger of *Time* writes, "an epidemic of any illness may be a terrible way to learn a lesson, but it's a decidedly effective one." People learn, especially when the facts hit them straight between the eyes.

4.1.3 Evolution of Species

In 2007, when asked if he believed in evolution, then–Republican presidential primary candidate Mike Huckabee replied, "I believe there is a God who was active in the creation process. Now, how did he do it, and when did he do it, and how long did he take? I don't honestly know." Huckabee continued, "If anybody wants to believe that they are the descendants of a primate, they are certainly welcome to do it."

Almost 150 years after Charles Darwin published *On the Origin of Species by Means of Natural Selection*, the notion that humans evolved from earlier primates over a long span of time is considered a part of the basics of modern science. However, as Huckabee's reply captures, for many Americans the debate over evolution continues.

Evolution is a well-established scientific theory that convincingly explains the origins and development of life on Earth. Most scientists hold the view, however, that such a scientific theory is not just a hunch or guess, but an established explanation for a natural phenomenon – like gravity – that has continuously been tested and supported by evidence. For practical purposes, evolution through natural selection is a fact.

So if evolution is as established as the theory of gravity, why are people still arguing about it a century and a half after it was first proposed? Part of the answer lies in the conflict between religion and science. The implications of believing in evolution by natural selection for people of certain religious inclinations are heretical, as they conflict with basic creationist teachings.

Since the early twentieth century, debates about evolution have carried into American politics where efforts have been made to ban evolution from being taught in public schools. These activists, often composed of evangelical Christiains, instead support the creationist theory of origin, which is drawn from stories in the Old Testament, in which God created the world in seven days. Sometimes referred to as "creation science" or "creationism," its proponents reject evolution as a valid explanation for how humans came to be.

The debate on what to teach in American public schools has frequently required intervention from the courts. In 1925 the state court decision in *The State of Tennessee* v. *John Thomas Scopes*, more often referred to as the Scopes "monkey" trial, protected a law prohibiting the teaching of evolution in the schools. However, a series of court rulings decades later restricted the ability of school boards and state governments to ban the teaching of evolution.

To navigate these court rulings, opponents of evolution began to target school curricula in more inventive ways. Some local and state school boards have considered teaching "intelligent design," a framework that posits that life is too complex to have developed without outside (divine) intervention. Another tactic by evolution opponents involved simply seeding doubt about evolution as a fact. For example, in the early 2000s a county in Georgia drew national attention for having stickers on biology textbooks with the line "Evolution is a theory, not a fact,

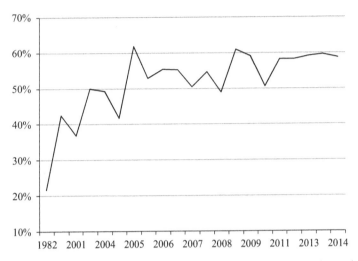

Figure 14 Percentage of Americans who are more likely to believe in evolution by natural selection (1982–2014)

Note: "Don't know" responses are dropped from analysis believe in evolution.
Source: Roper Center for Public Opinion Research

concerning the origin of living things." Parents eventually filed a lawsuit against Cobb County and and ultimately a federal judge ruled the stickers unconstitutional.

Given this historic and continuing debate within school boards, states, and courts on whether or not to teach evolution in public schools, what does the public think? Figure 14 plots the percentage of Americans who report that they are more likely to believe in the theory of evolution (as opposed to other theories). A cursory scan of the graph indicates a strong upward trend. In 1982, when asked "Do you agree more with the theory of evolution or more with the theory of creationism?" fewer than a quarter of Americans said evolution. When we move to 2014, just shy of two-thirds of Americans reported they are more likely to believe in evolution.

The figure shows a remarkable shift in public perception, converging toward facts. We speculate why. One potential explanation is Americans' declining religiosity. In 1976, 38 percent of Americans believed the Bible to be the literal word of God. In 2017, only 24 percent of Americans did, a record low historically.[28] Because of this decline, fewer people face the internal conflict that believing in evolution creates for those with strong religious beliefs. In turn, there are more Americans who will not reject scientific consensus on the basis of religious reasons and in turn are more receptive to the facts.

---

[28] Data from Gallup.

A second possibility for why we see a shift toward the facts involves generational replacement and educational standards. State efforts to legally ban the teaching of evolution were blocked by a 9–0 Supreme Court decision in *Epperson* v. *Arkansas* in 1968. Since then, efforts to ban teaching evolution continue, but they face tough barriers. Dozens of states have set academic standards that require evolution to be an included class curriculum. Further, at least twenty states include evolution as a topic covered in state tests, where creationism is not.[29] In other words, increasingly students around the country are required to take exams where the presumption is that evolution is *the* correct explanation for species origin and development. Thus, students are on the receiving end of the information flow and have an incentive to be receptive to the facts. These changes in educational standards should have implications for what Americans believe over time. We expect that given that these educational standards remain, as new cohorts of voters emerge and older cohorts fade away, public acceptance of evolution will continue.

The case of evolution is informative to our understanding of the role of facts in public opinion in several ways. It demonstrates the capacity of government to identify what is fact and what is false, and pass policy based on that knowledge. Effectively, government can promote factual learning. It also speaks to the role of motivation (beyond belief perseverance) in the reporting of facts. We know monetary incentives successfully motivate citizens to report the facts (Prior & Lupia, 2008). Similarly, through state exams that have identified evolution as a fact, generation after generation of students should also be motivated to learn the facts.

4.1.4 Climate Change

In our concluding section of scientific facts, we turn to climate change. As we saw in Section 1, by the 1980s the principal scientific questions were settled. The Earth was warming at a rate never seen before, as a result of humans burning fossil fuels. A scientific consensus emerged. Soon afterward, scientific attention transitioned from an accurate diagnosis of the problem to understanding the consequences and identifying possible solutions.

Several important events happened in the decades that followed. In 1988, NASA's James Hansen testified before the Senate – despite efforts by the White House to silence him – on the dangers of global warming, citing certain significant changes that had already begun. Following the hearing, a bipartisan coalition of senators pushed for legislation to address climate change and called for President Reagan to sign an international treaty aimed

---

[29] Sean Cavanagh, *Education Week* (December 5, 2005).

at reducing carbon emissions. Their efforts did not prove fruitful. Once George H. W. Bush took office, White House officials directly questioned the scientific merits of the predictions Hansen and other scientists had made.[30] The Bush administration would end up promoting no momentous policy shifts and would actually actively discredited climate scientists.[31]

Since the early 1990s, partisan elites have begun to more clearly sort out environmental issues, whereby the two major parties, funded by different interest groups and corporations, better established their support of and opposition to policies that recognized the reality of climate change. The public debate gained more steam after President Clinton signed the Kyoto Protocol in 1997, followed by a refusal of ratification from the Republican-held Senate. Since then, there has been the predictable back and forth on climate change between partisans. From George W. Bush's withdrawal of America's signature from the Kyoto Protocol, to President Barack Obama's signing of the Paris Agreement, to President Trump's withdrawal from the agreement, the United States continues to flip-flop on climate change.

Though consistently a divisive topic for politicians, climate change often has taken a back seat on the political agenda relative to other issues. However, enough political and media attention to the issue has made the public increasingly aware of the problem (Egan & Mullin, 2017). And starting in the late 1990s, pollsters began ask to Americans about their views on climate change with consistent frequency.

The factual debate about climate change has been in public discourse for decades and is substantiated by strong evidence, clearly rewarding one side. However, unlike most issues we address in this Element, the facts are unavoidably multi-faceted. First, there is the question of whether climate change is even occurring. And if so, when? Why? How much certainty do scientists have? In what follows, we illustrate long-term public opinion on each of these factually based facets of the issue.

To track over time public opinion on climate change, we combine survey data that rely on survey questions with nearly identical wording over time, sometimes from the same survey house and sometimes from multiple ones. Data availability limitations lead us to have some relatively short time series.

We start with the most basic scientific question of this debate: Is global warming happening? In other terms, is the Earth's average temperature increasing at an abnormal rate? The percentage of the American public that says yes to this question over an almost ten-year time interval (2009–2018) is shown in

---

[30] Nathanial Rich, The Next Reckoning: Capitalism and Climate Change, *New York Times Magazine* (April 29, 2018)

[31] However, in 1992 Bush did sign a United Nations treaty on climate change. This treaty, however, did not come close to addressing the problem.

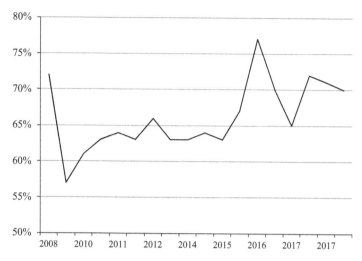

Figure 15 Percentage of Americans reporting that "global warming is happening" (2009–2018)

Source: Roper Center for Public Opinion Research

Figure 15. We see a sudden fifteen-point drop in the percentage of people who believe global warming is happening from October of 2008 to January 2010. But throughout Obama's tenure as president, belief in climate change steadily rises. On average, we observe an upward trend converging toward the facts.

So if Americans are more likely than not to believe that global warming is happening, when will we feel the effects? Figure 16 plots the percentage of Americans who report that the effects of global warming have already begun from 1997 through 2017. On average we observe an upward trend. At its peak near the end of each series, two-thirds of Americans say that global warming is happening and we are experiencing the effects of it *now.*

At the elite level, there seems to be some consensus that changes in the Earth's climate are happening. Where the real debate lies for politics are the causes and how to address them. Given that the scientific consensus is that global warming is a result of human activity, where does the public stand? The percentage of the public from 2011 to 2018 that believes global warming is caused by human activity is shown in Figure 17. We see that the aggregate opinion on average trends upward, converging toward facts.

One of the ways in which political elites promoted and sustained doubt in the minds of Americans was to push the idea that climate change was still part of a scientific debate, downplaying the actual consensus that had long been established by experts. If the facts are established, we would expect the public to pick up on the existence of a consensus among the factual experts. Figure 18

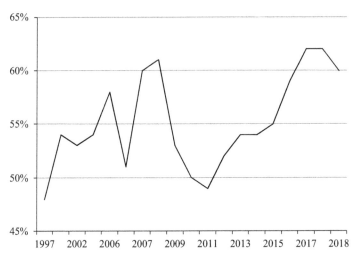

Figure 16 Percentage of Americans reporting that the effects of global warming
have already begun (1997–2018)

Source: Gallup

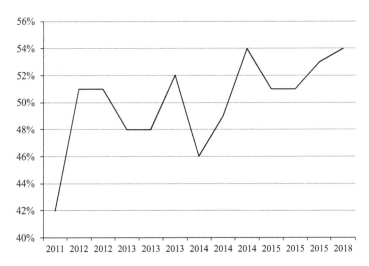

Figure 17 Percentage of Americans reporting that "global warming is caused
mostly by human activity such as burning fossil fuels" (2011–2018)

Source: CBS/NYT polls

shows the percentage of the public that agrees with the statement "most
scientists believe that global warming is occuring" over a twenty-year interval.
We see some cyclical movement; however, the public's belief in a consensus

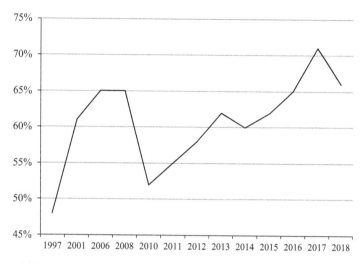

Figure 18 Percentage of Americans reporting that "most scientists believe that global warming is occurring"

Source: Gallup

peaks toward the end of the series, suggesting an overall trend converging toward the facts.

When we observe how aggregate opinion moves on various components of the factual debate on climate change – its existence, immediacy, causes, and underlying scientific consensus – we interpret this movement as slowly trending toward the facts. Some readers will doubt our interpretation. Indeed, other scholars have interpreted these over time fluctuations in aggregate opinion as having little meaning (Egan & Mullin, 2017). What is apparent, however, is that when we compare the beginning to the end of each series, there is no strong backward trend: aggregate opinion does not move far *away* from the facts as the public debate continues.

So what accounts for the shifts in the aggregate opinion observed over time? As many have documented, the partisan polarization on climate change at the elite level has trickled down to the electorate. Elites on the right have political incentives to keep their voters misinformed on climate change (Hochschild & Einstein, 2015b). In turn, liberals are far more likely than conservatives to believe the facts on climate change.

But accuracy goals may overcome directional goals when factual information is continuously and clearly repeated over time. As we saw in Section 1, the way in which partisans react to new information is surprisingly consistent with the ideal of Bayesian rationality. People will move in the accurate direction when they receive signals so numerous and visible that their prior beliefs are overwhelmed, and they begin to rationally update.

We expect that in the case of climate change, the public has moved toward the facts due to the high quality and quantity of information it has received. Consensus among climate scientists has been translated in American media coverage, where dissenting opinions about the reality of climate change are contextualized as fringe perspectives (Brüggemann & Engesser, 2017). Further, as the devastating effects of climate change are becoming more apparent, both these events and coverage of them are being signaled to Americans. Although voters are exposed to copious amounts of competing signals, these highly visible facts should be reinforced through repetition over time to the point where remaining noise is drowned out.

4.2 Real-World Trends

We now move away from established scientific facts and look to how competent Americans are when it comes to learning about facts involving numbers and trends. In Section 2, we saw that on average the public responds to the economy over time and picks up on changing tides. However, the economy is unique in that it is consistently reported as among the most important issues in American politics. Signals about the status of the economy are everywhere. We shift gears here and look to trends that are perhaps less central to voters' views of public affairs, but prominent enough that we expect they should be able to follow the facts.

4.2.1 Economic Inequality

Income inequality has received growing attention from political elites and scholars in recent years. Though inequality has increased markedly over the past several decades in the United States, we have not observed the increases in voter demands for redistributive policies that popular economic models would predict (Kelly & Enns, 2010). Some scholars attribute this failure to connect rising inequality with the appropriate policies in part to Americans being too ignorant or failing to pay attention (Bartels, 2008). We agree with pessimists that citizens are unlikely to be able to estimate levels of inequality at single cross sections in time. But, overall, have they really failed to see that inequality is rising over time?

To answer, we compare over time changes in national income inequality and public opinion. To illustrate levels of inequality, we plot the percentage of total income held by the top 1 percent of income earners for each year from 1969 to 2015 in Figure 19.[32] While there are several ways to estimate economic

---

[32] Data provided by the US Census March Supplement studies.

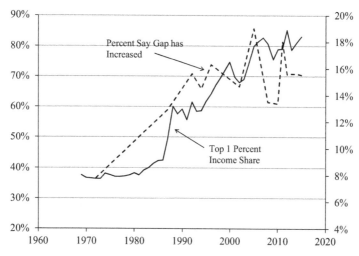

Figure 19 Top 1 percent income share (right axis) and percentage of Americans reporting that the gap between the rich and poor has increased (left axis) (1972–2015)

Note: "Don't know" responses are dropped from analysis.

Source: US Census and Roper Center for Public Opinion Research

inequality, rising income disparities are largely a result of the rapid expansion of incomes at the top of the income distribution (Piketty, 2017). While survey data on inequality are sparse, particularly in the 1970s and 1980s, we still see it useful to track over time changes. The series for public opinion (1972–2015) is the percentage of survey respondents who report that the gap between the rich and poor has increased.

Looking at the graph, it appears that as income inequality has increased, the portion of the public that reports this gap as either wide or growing has also increased. We calculated the simple product moment correlations between public perception and levels of national inequality, resulting in a correlation of 0.86.[33] We need to be wary that accidental correlation can occur between two unrelated time series, both of which have a linear trend. But actual inequality and perceived inequality are hardly unrelated. We were surprised that this correlation was as high as it was, but we take it with a grain of salt, acknowledging the sparsity of opinion data on this subject. Though there is a weaker consensus on the question of if and how government should address this trend, our question is more limited: Does the mass public follow the facts? The answer is yes.

---

[33] Values for years where opinion data were missing were interpolated.

4.2.2 Crime

Often we hear that Americans' perceptions of crime are at odds with the reality. Reports of inaccurate perceptions, with headlines such as "Most Americans don't know the truth about crime" (*The Washington Post*), create a picture of an electorate that has an inflated perception of actual crime. We wanted to know, though, if this has always been the case. We do not expect Americans to estimate with any accuracy the true crime rate. But we do expect that it can sense when crime is going up and when it is going down.

Since 1972, Gallup has regularly asked Americans: "Is there more crime in this area than there was a year ago, or less?" Using Gallup's time series, we plot the percentage of Americans who say there is more crime.[34] To see how closely the ups and downs of perceptions of crime follow real-world trends, we also gathered actual crime rates. The FBI crime databank breaks down crime rates by different types of crime: murder, robbery, aggravated assault, and rape.

First, we compare perception of increases in crime to the national murder rate. A look at Figure 20 shows that for the first thirty years of the series, perception of crime and actual crime trend together to some degree. When the murder rate

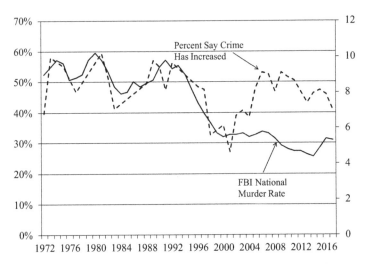

Figure 20 The FBI murder rate (right axis) and percentage of Americans saying crime in their area has increased (left axis) (1972–2017)

Note: "Don't know" responses are dropped from analysis.

Source: FBI Official Crime Statistics and Gallup

---

[34] We compute this percentage by dividing the percentage who say there is more crime by the sum of those who say there is more crime, those who say there is less crime, and those who say crime has stayed the same. "Don't know" responses are dropped from the analysis.

goes up, the portion of the public that believes crime has increased also goes up. However, in the early 2000s we begin to see a mismatch: as the murder rate steadily declined, perception of crime increasing went up. The trend we see in the 2000s onward fits the narrative we commonly hear today. But the trend for the first thirty years suggests that the public was able to follow the facts.

We were interested in exactly when this deviation between perception and reality began. A statistical test for a structural break in the relationship between the two series suggested a break in the year 2000. The product moment correlation between public perception and the murder rate from 1972 to 2000 is .82.[35] However, when we consider the series as a whole (1972–2017), the correlation between crime perception and murder rate is a more modest .54.

But why do we see this divergence in the early 2000s? We consider several possibilities. First, a common narrative evoked among academics is that the news media exaggerate crime. Why? Violent crime is a headline. Absence of crime is not. This differs from moving target facts such as the economy. Good or bad, the state of the economy is always reported on. Crime will always get more emphasis than no crime at all. So the media over-report violent crime, but this has been true since the 1970s.

Thus, this explanation alone cannot account for the divergence we see in the early 2000s. Beginning in the early twenty-first century, we also have seen significant advancements in the way people consume news (24/7 news cycle, the Internet, the prominence of smart phone devices) that have changed the way we learn about the world. Combine a media that consistently over-reports crime with the way in which news is ever-present in our lives, and the result is a public with a heightened perception of crime.

Finally, there has been a shift in the nature of violent crimes. While the average homicide rate in the United States has steadily declined for the past couple of decades, the fatalities that have resulted from mass shootings have increased. Of the the thirty-eight deadliest mass shootings in American history since 1949, twenty-four (63 percent) of them occured between 2000 and 2019. Couple this with the fact that the deadliest terrorist attack on US soil was on September 11, 2001. With high-profile tragedies such as these, is it unreasonable for more Americans to believe crime is growing?

Our analysis of crime is not without its limitations. Our measure of crime perception is flawed in that the survey question we rely on is exceedingly vague. "Crime" can have a multitude of meanings. For some it will bring up images of mass shootings. For others it may bring up images of aggravated assault. When we conduct the same analysis described for other types of crime (rape, robbery,

---

[35] Values for years where opinion data were missing were interpolated.

and assault), there is a weak relationship between perception and actual crime. However, the rate of specific crimes – murder, rape, robbery, assault – do not trend in exact parallel. It would therefore be impossible for the public to "get it right" for all types of crimes when we only rely on one survey question.

So what can we conclude about the public and crime? We see some signs of learning, but it is imperfect. In the following sections, we explore other pathological cases where there is mixed or counter evidence that the public learns.

4.3 Pathologies: When Opinion Does Not Follow the Facts

So far we have presented several cases where we see mass opinion absorb the facts surprisingly well. In the long term, these cases present us with a public where facts have greater leverage on opinion than falsehoods. This is evident in the convergence toward facts of aggregate opinion, as well as the public's tendency to follow real-world trends with relative accuracy. In this section we bring attention to cases where public opinion does not converge on facts.

4.3.1 Voter Fraud

The public debate surrounding voter identification laws has not gained as much leverage on facts as we would expect. While it is one of the most contentious issues in recent years among political elites, a strong partisan divide is hardly visible among the public, where voter ID laws enjoy broad support from voters across partisan lines (Daprile, 2015). It is an established fact that the fraud such laws aim to deter occurs at a minuscule frequency.[36] Yet, laws requiring a form of photo identification remain popular. This popularity is a consequence of many factors, but similar to other laws requiring identification, it is likely to be informed in some way by a perception that such laws effectively deter fraud. A 2016 poll by the Associated Press found that 60 percent of Americans thought that there was either "some" or a "great deal" of instances of voter fraud. In early 2018, a Pew poll found that more than 80 percent of Americans endorsed the statement "voter fraud across the US has undermined the results of our elections." It appears that facts here do not have quite the pull we would expect.

So why do we not see convergence on the facts (yet)? There are several possibilities. First, as the debate over voter fraud and voter identification laws began to gain steam, the aftermath of the 2016 presidential election also ignited debate over the sanctity of the American election process. Following the 2016 election, intelligence authorities confirmed that the Russian government interfered in the

---

[36] From 2000 to 2014, credible instances of voter impersonation in the United States occurred a total of 31 times (Levitt, 2014).

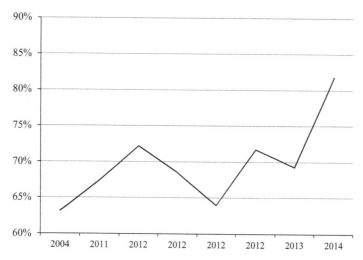

Figure 21 Percentage of Americans saying that voter fraud is prevalent
(2004–2014)
Source: Roper Center for Public Opinion Research

election in an effort to spark political instability and damage Hillary Clinton's run for president. Russians accomplished this by spreading misinformation through online social media platforms and hacking the Democratic National Committee's databases. Moreover, Russian operatives also hacked into some states' electronic election systems. But how is this relevant to people's opinions on voter identification laws? It is possible that when respondents today were asked about voter fraud following 2016, they were not just thinking about voter impersonation – they could have been considering the *multiple* ways in which American elections had been tampered with. And for the most part, Americans have come to recognize that Russians interfered in the 2016 election (see Figure 22).[37] Thus, we cannot be certain that Americans' perceptions of voter fraud are grounded in a similar frame of reference. So though we concede that public perceptions of actual voter fraud have not converged toward facts, we remain a bit dubious of the long-term trend we do observe (see Figure 21).

Another possibility as to why we do not see a convergence toward facts is related to government policy. State legislatures have increasingly proposed and passed measures requiring forms of identification to vote (Hicks, McKee, Sellers, & Smith, 2015). If we take laws as protective measures, these laws send a message to voters: required voter identification is necessary to shield elections from voter fraud. They insinuate the existence of a problem by means

---

[37] The trend in this figure is not statistically significant, but with only four cases that is not a surprise.

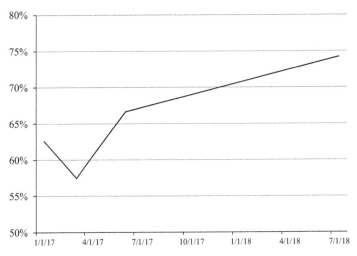

Figure 22 Percentage of Americans reporting that Russia interfered with the 2016 election (2017–2018)

Source: Roper Center for Public Opinion Research

of presenting a solution. Thus a reasonable person might ask, if voter imperso-nation does *not* occur, why would public officials go to all the trouble of passing laws that deter it? The politically sophisticated may be more tuned into the underlying partisan motivations of those who advocate for voter ID laws. But for the majority of voters, these relatively new and prominent laws send a signal. So while we have noted that laws have considerable power to motivate the acceptance of fact, there is the possibility of the opposite effect: government policy can send signals that promote false beliefs among the public.

Some of the problem of the voter fraud case is that the correct fact is a negative, voter impersonation fraud rarely occurs. It would be easy to assert the positive case. The evidence would be frequent and successful prosecutions of those caught in impersonation. It is clearly against the law. But to argue against widespread fraud one would have to know that such prosecutions are rare. Ordinary citizens would have to hang out at the local courthouse to acquire such information. Imagine the headline: "Today no one was prosecuted for voter impersonation fraud."

4.3.2 Estimating Figures

Voter fraud of course is not the only issue plagued by factual misperceptions. Other issues – such as government spending and the size of certain populations, are also susceptible to misperceptions (Gilens, 2001; Sides & Citrin, 2007). However, limited data availability across time does not leave us with much to

Table 5 Public perception of government spending

Year	Food Stamps	Foreign Aid	Medicare	Social Security	Defense
1997	26	64	23	50	56
2004	23	49	25	26	51
2005	10	39	20	33	73
2009	17	45	33	33	54
2010	23	40	35	29	49

Note: Respondents were asked: "Which of the items on this list would you say are the two largest areas of spending by the federal government … defense, food stamps, foreign aid, Medicare, Social Security. (If more than two, ask:) If you could only choose 2 items from this list–which would you choose?" Percentages do not add to 100.
Source: Roper Center for Public Opinion Research

interpret. For example, large sections of the public consistently report defense spending as occupying one of the top priorities for the federal budget, which is correct. However, they also believe foreign aid is a top area of government spending, which it is not (see Table 6). Though actual foreign aid spending hovers around 1 percent to 2 percent of the total federal budget, recent estimates suggest that on average the public believes that about a quarter of the budget is dedicated to foreign aid.[38] Pessimistic scholars might attribute this to simple ignorance. But expecting ordinary Americans to know what portion of the budget is spent on various programs is a tall order. We must ask ourselves: Are we questioning Americans on facts we expect they should follow, or are we simply testing them on "information that academics, journalists, and politicos value" (Lupia, 2006, p. 218).

A deeper look into public opinion on government expenditures paints a more complex picture than an ignorant electorate incapable of learning. By conducting a qualitative analysis of open-ended interviews with ordinary people, Williamson (2018) finds that conceptions of what actually qualifies as foreign aid vary widely. In contrast to the definition followed by policy makers or scholars, many people consider military spending as a type of overseas spending, and those who define foreign aid in these terms are more likely to perceive it as a large share of the budget. Williamson's study suggests that for us to better understand what Americans know, we must consider the words, frames, and concepts people use to come to certain factual understandings.

---

[38] Survey by the Henry J. Kaiser Family Foundation. December 2–December 9, 2014.

The pathologies we have discussed so far – voter fraud rates, population and spending estimates – share a common feature in that they demonstrate the public's political innumeracy, which involves the inability to understand risk, probabilistic, or mathematical concepts. According to the National Adult Literacy Survey, about half of Americans lack minimal quantitative skills or are "innumerate." For politically relevant facts, this hinders average people's ability to estimate certain numeric figures and think abstractly.

Political innumeracy should not come as a surprise to us. Large numbers and statistics lie outside people's everyday experience. They are abstract concepts that require attention to detail; at a certain point, the average person understandably gets lost: millions become billions and billions become trillions. Further, for the public to get the facts right, a strong information stream is required. However, high-quality information about specific federal budget appropriations is not found daily on the front page of the average person's local newspaper. So the public may not be able to report accurate estimates for government spending or certain populations: but given what it is exposed to, should we expect it to?

Consider an example. As we saw earlier, in 2015, more than two-thirds of Americans reported that the gap between the rich and poor is increasing. However, when asked how much more CEOs are paid than the average pay of a company worker, the majority (46 percent) of respondents said ten times more. Only 6 percent of Americans said 200 times more, which is closest to the correct answer.[39] We do see that Americans have learned that income inequality is becoming increasingly severe. By precisely how much, however, average folks do not know.

4.4 Conclusion

"The Earth Is Flat." Reading those four words causes most of us a sense of astonishment. Didn't we learn early in our elementary school years that Christopher Columbus had the opposite idea and discovered the Americas while searching for a route to India? So how could anybody say such a thing?[40] The Earth is flat. Smoking presents no risk to health. Vaccines cause children to develop autism. Global climate is the same for all time. God created the Earth in seven days. All these things have a "man bites dog" aspect. In a century that glories in science and technology, it is highly unexpected that anyone holds such beliefs.

Men do not very often bite dogs. But when they do, we can be sure that it will be noted and that we, the public, will hear about it. Dogs do very often bite men.

---

[39] Survey by CBS News, September 28–October 2, 2016.
[40] We need to reserve the possibility that some flat-Earthers are having a little fun at our expense.

It is anything but astonishing; it is expected. And so when it happens we are assumed to not be interested and thus it often goes unreported. Who cares?

And so it goes when scholars and journalists write about the facts that Americans know or do not know. We are astonished that a very small number of Americans believe in a flat Earth and so we write about it. We are not astonished that most Americans learned their grade school lessons about Columbus. And by this logic we can understand why failure to process facts gets more emphasis than dull success. But what we see when we look at issue after issue – granted, with exceptions – is that dull success is the norm.

5 How Much Does the Public Know: An Assessment of Knowledge and Learning

Assessment of how much mass publics know about various topics is usually seen as a cross-sectional question. We ask a question: Does smoking cause cancer? And then we do a survey and discover that x percent assert a belief that the causal story is true or false. This is obviously a reasonable way to proceed.

But whatever the percentage correct turns out to be, it misses the important fact that constroversies are a process. The answer that we find is not true for all time but instead reflects the point at which we observe the contest.

Our view of factual learning, more or less an accidental by-product of our theory, is that factual controversies are typically episodes. While facts themselves might be eternal, factual controversies are events dated in time. They have discernible beginnings and ends. They begin when some controversial claim is made in the public space. And they continue while others add claims and counterclaims. And then they end when the fiery initial question leads to a boring consensus conclusion. Once almost everybody believes the same thing, the episode is over. And we will go on to contest something else.

The climate change episode, our opening example, can be said to have its beginning sometime in the late 1970s and early 1980s when climate scientists became so concerned about their findings that they began to need public involvement in what was then a scientific debate about theory, evidence, and conclusion. Scientists themselves could not alter public policy, particularly on a global scale. To do that the debate had to involve millions of ordinary people. Its end is not in sight. But we will know that we have reached it when public opinion reflects the consensus that is already in place among scientists. The Watergate episode was more easily defined. It lasted from roughly January 1973 to the August 1974 end of the Nixon presidency. The smoking and cancer controversy is similarly dead, not from cancer, but from consensus that smoking is dangerous.

Our most important claim in this Element is that episodes have a direction. Beliefs change over time and information flows toward the facts. And that change cannot be seen in cross-sectional views. However, we must qualify our claims. First, we concede that the rate of change toward facts varies across factual debates, sometimes at a glacial pace that may be of little comfort to readers. We did not, however, write this Element with the intention of offering comfort. There is no denying that falsehoods and misperceptions have the capacity to present severe risks to public health, policy, and democracy. And if the public is too slow moving toward the facts, these risks are heightened. Instead we hope to contextualize factual debates, illustrate how they evolve, and demonstrate that the public has a stronger capacity to learn than it often gets credit for.

Second, we cannot predict precisely when public opinion will converge toward the facts. We assert only that it eventually will. For factual debates that have "ended" (they are no longer a source of public debate), our prediction is simple to test. But for factual debates that are ongoing, our expectation is difficult to disprove. We will always have another day ahead.

Lastly, we only claim that the public will learn for factual cases where there has been controversy. It has often been observed that the American public is not strong on constitutional facts about American politics. How many years is a senator's term? How many members serve in the House of Representatives? We get some perspective on facts like these by noting that they lack public controversy. Learning occurs during episodes of controversy. That is what drives its essential information flow. There is no controversy about Senate terms or House seats. Without controversy there are no episodes – and no episodic learning.

So yes, the public does learn when there are episodes of controversy over facts. But public controversy over facts is spotty. Some facts are contested while others are not. In the end, a good brawl produces a more informed public.

5.1 Reconciliation

We wrote in Section 1 that we joined the scholarly consensus that mass electorates are not, in general, well informed. We believe that ordinary people invest their time in learning things they find important to daily life. And we believe that public affairs only rarely take a place in that category. Thus we expect to find factual ignorance more widespread than factual knowledge.

And now we have written in these last sections that ordinary citizens, exposed to controversy about facts, do learn. So how do we reconcile a learning public with an ignorant one? The key to reconciling these apparently discrepant facts is this: most factual issues are *not* subject to public controversy. The number of facts – and potential issues about facts – is uncountably large. The number of factual controversies is very small. The bandwidth of public debate is narrow. That is because there is insufficient public interest to sustain multiple debates at any one time.

The potential for public learning is always with us. But if 99 out of 100 potential controversies remain on the sidelines of public attention, then that potential is rarely realized. And so we conclude: (1) the public learns, and (2) nonetheless, it is not well informed.

References

Barkun, M. (2013). *A culture of conspiracy: Apocalyptic visions in contemporary America*. Berkeley: University of California Press.

Bartels, L. M. (2002). Beyond the running tally: Partisan bias in political perceptions. *Political Behavior, 24*(2), 117–50.

(2008). *Unequal democracy: The political economy of the new gilded age*. Princeton: Princeton University Press.

Berelson, B. R., Lazarsfeld, P. F., & McPhee, W. N. (1954). *Voting: A study of opinion formation in a presidential campaign*. Chicago: University of Chicago Press.

Berinsky, A. J. (2007). Assuming the costs of war: Events, elites, and American public support for military conflict. *The Journal of Politics, 69*(4), 975–97.

Brüggemann, M., & Engesser, S. (2017). Beyond false balance: How interpretive journalism shapes media coverage of climate change. *Global Environmental Change, 42*, 58–67.

Campbell, A., Converse, P. E., Miller, W. E., & Stokes, D. E. (1960). *The American voter*. New York: Wiley.

Coppock, A. E. (2016). Positive, small, homogeneous, and durable: Political persuasion in response to information. Doctoral Dissertation. Columbia University.

Daprile, L. (June 2015). *Scott walker says most Americans support voter ID laws, which make it easier to vote*. Retrieved from www.politifact.com/

Darwin, C. (1859). *On the origins of species by means of natural selection*. London: Murray.

Delli Carpini, M. X., & Keeter, S. (1996). *What Americans know about politics and why it matters*. New Haven: Yale University Press.

Derthick, Martha A. (2011). *Up in smoke: From legislation to litigation in tobacco politics*. Sage.

Downs, A. (1957). *An economic theory of democracy*. New York: Harper and Row.

Druckman, J. N. (2012). The politics of motivation. *Critical Review, 24*(2), 199–216.

Durkin, Sarah & Emily Brennan & Melanie Wakefield. (2012). Mass media campaigns to promote smoking cessation among adults: an integrative review. *Tobacco Control*, 21(2), 127–138.

Egan, P. J., & Mullin, M. (2017). Climate change: US public opinion. *Annual Review of Political Science, 20*, 209–27.

Faris, R., Roberts, H., Etling, B., Bourassa, N., Zuckerman, E., & Benkler, Y. (2017). Partisanship, propaganda, and disinformation: Online media and the 2016 us presidential election. *Berkman Klein Center for Internet Society Research Paper.*

Gaines, B. J., Kuklinski, J. H., Quirk, P. J., Peyton, B., & Verkuilen, J. (2007). Same facts, different interpretations: Partisan motivation and opinion on Iraq. *Journal of Politics, 69*(4), 957–74.

Garrett, R. K. (2011). Troubling consequences of online political rumoring. *Human Communication Research, 37*(2), 255–74.

Gerber, A., & Green, D. P. (1998). Rational learning and partisan attitudes. *American Journal of Political Science, 42*(3), 794–818.

Gilens, M. (2001). Political ignorance and collective policy preferences. *American Political Science Review, 95*(2), 379–96.

Guess, A., & Coppock, A. (2018). Does counter-attitudinal information cause backlash? Results from three large survey experiments. *British Journal of Political Science,* 1–19. DOI:https://doi.org/10.1017/S0007123418000327

Guess, A., Nyhan, B., & Reifler, J. (2018). Selective exposure to misinformation: Evidence from the consumption of fake news during the 2016 US presidential campaign. *European Research Council, 9.*

Hicks, W. D., McKee, S. C., Sellers, M. D., & Smith, D. A. (2015). A principle or a strategy? Voter identification laws and partisan competition in the American states. *Political Research Quarterly, 68*(1), 18–33.

Hill, S. J. (2017). Learning together slowly: Bayesian learning about political facts. *The Journal of Politics, 79*(4), 1403–18.

Hochschild, J., & Einstein, K. L. (2015a). It isn't what we don't know that gives us trouble, it's what we know that ain't so: Misinformation and democratic politics. *British Journal of Political Science, 45*(3), 467–75.

(2015b). *Do facts matter? Information and misinformation in American politics.* Norman: University of Oklahoma Press.

Hopkins, D. J., Sides, J., & Citrin, J. (2019). The muted consequences of correct information about immigration. *The Journal of Politics, 81*(1), 315–20.

Ingber, S. (1984). The marketplace of ideas: A legitimizing myth. *Duke Law Journal, 33*(1), 6–91.

Jerit, J., & Barabas, J. (2006). Bankrupt rhetoric: How misleading information affects knowledge about Social Security. *Public Opinion Quarterly, 70*(3), 278–303.

(2012). Partisan perceptual bias and the information environment. *The Journal of Politics, 74*(3), 672–84.

Kelly, N. J., & Enns, P. K. (2010). Inequality and the dynamics of public opinion: The self-reinforcing link between economic inequality and mass preferences. *American Journal of Political Science, 54*(4), 855–70.

Kuklinski, J. H., & Quirk, P. J. (2000). Reconsidering the rational public: Cognition, heuristics, and mass opinion. Lupia, Arthur & Mathew McCubbins & Samuel Popkin, eds. *Elements of reason: Cognition, choice, and the bounds of rationality*, 153–82, Cambridge University Press.

Kunda, Z. (1990). The case for motivated reasoning. *Psychological Bulletin, 108*(3), 480–98.

Lavine, H. G., Johnston, C. D., & Steenbergen, M. R. (2012). *The ambivalent partisan: How critical loyalty promotes democracy*. Oxford University Press, New York.

Levitt, J. (2014). A comprehensive investigation of voter impersonation finds 31 credible incidents out of one billion ballots cast. Retrieved from www.washing tonpost.com/news/wonk/wp/2014/08/06/a-comprehensive-investigation-of-voter-impersonation-finds-31-credible-incidents-out-of-one-billion-ballots-cast/

Lupia, A. (2006). How elitism undermines the study of voter competence. *Critical Review, 18*(1–3), 217–32.

Lupia, A., & McCubbins, M. D. (1998). *The democratic dilemma: Can citizens learn what they need to know?* Cambridge, UK; New York: Cambridge University Press.

Nyhan, Brendan & Jason Reifler (2010). When Perceptions Fail: The Persistence of Political Misperceptions. *Political Behavior, 32*(2) 303–330.

Olive, J. K., Hotez, P. J., Damania, A., & Nolan, M. S. (2018). The state of the antivaccine movement in the United States: A focused examination of nonmedical exemptions in states and counties. *PLoS Medicine, 15*(6), e1002578.

Page, B. I., & Shapiro, R. Y. (1992). *The rational public: Fifty years of trends in Americans' policy preferences*. Chicago: University of Chicago Press.

Parker-Stephen, E. (2007). Learning about change: Information, motivation, and political perception. Doctoral Dissertation. University of North Carolina at Chapel Hill.

(2013). Tides of disagreement: How reality facilitates (and inhibits) partisan public opinion. *The Journal of Politics, 75*(4), 1077–88.

Pasek, J., Stark, T. H., Krosnick, J. A., Tompson, T., & Payne, B. K. (2014). Attitudes toward Blacks in the Obama era: Changing distributions and impacts on job approval and electoral choice, 2008–2012. *Public Opinion Quarterly, 78*(S1), 276–302.

Petrocik, J. R. (1996). Issue ownership in presidential elections, with a 1980 case study. *American Journal of Political Science*, 825–50.

Piketty, T. (2017). *Capital in the twenty-first century*. Cambridge, MA: Harvard University Press.

Prior, M., & Lupia, A. (2008). Money, time, and political knowledge: Distinguishing quick recall and political learning skills. *American Journal of Political Science*, *52*(1), 169–83.

Redlawsk, D. P., Civettini, A. J., & Emmerson, K. M. (2010). The affective tipping point: Do motivated reasoners ever get it? *Political Psychology, 31* (4), 563–93.

Sides, J., & Citrin, J. (2007). European opinion about immigration: The role of identities, interests and information. *British Journal of Political Science, 37*(3), 477–504.

Stimson, J. A. (2015). *Tides of consent: How public opinion shapes American politics*, rev. 2nd ed. New York; London: Cambridge University Press.

Stroud, N. J. (2008). Media use and political predispositions: Revisiting the concept of selective exposure. *Political Behavior, 30*(3), 341–66.

Taber, C. S., & Lodge, M. (2006). Motivated skepticism in the evaluation of political beliefs. *American Journal of Political Science, 50*(3), 755–69.

Wood, T., & Porter, E. (2019). The elusive backfire effect: Mass attitudes' steadfast factual adherence. *Political Behavior, 41*(1), 135–63.

Zaller, J. R. (1992). *The nature and origins of mass opinions*. New York: Cambridge University Press.

Zaller, J., & Feldman, S. (1992). A simple theory of the survey response: Answering questions and revealing preferences. *American Journal of Political Science, 36*, 579–616.

Acknowledgments

We are grateful for the advice of several individuals, without whom this Element would be lesser. Lisa Sloan guided us through climate science with an insider's perspective. John Bullock intervened at a critical juncture to offer guidance on theory.

We owe a large debt of gratitude to the Department of Political Science at University of North Carolina Chapel Hill, the intellectual cradle within which our collaboration flourished. The Raymond Dawson Endowment supported both of us during the creation of this Element. Emily was partially supported by a NSF grant (SES-1841184). As is true of most of what is written about macro public opinion, the work would not be possible without the excellent work of the Roper Center for Public Opinion Research at Cornell University.

Individuals who have helped along the way – some without knowing it – include Brenden Nyhan, Nate Kelly, David Peterson, Jennifer Jerit, Frank Baumgartner, Derek Epp, Andrea Benjamin, Emily Thorson, Matt Jarvis, Lauren Elliot-Dorans, Leah Christiani, Jelle Koedam, Dave Attewell, and Eroll Kuhn.

Cambridge University Press has supplied an activist editor, Frances Lee, who has improved the Element in numerous regards. We are thankful also to Pat Egan and an anonymous reviewer for Cambridge for detailed and thoughtful critiques of the manuscript. Sara Doskow helped out in the early days by encouraging the research program that became this Element. Any errors are ours alone.

Cambridge Elements ⹀

American Politics

Francis E. Lee

Princeton University

Frances E. Lee is Professor of Politics at the Woodrow Wilson School of Princeton University. She is author of *Insecure Majorities: Congress and the Perpetual Campaign* (2016), *Beyond Ideology: Politics, Principles and Partisanship in the U.S. Senate* (2009), and coauthor of *Sizing Up the Senate: The Unequal Consequences of Equal Representation* (1999).

Advisory Board

About the Series

The Cambridge Elements Series in *American Politics* publishes authoritative contributions on American politics. Emphasizing works that address big, topical questions within the American political landscape, the series is open to all branches of the subfield and actively welcomes works that bridge subject domains. It publishes both original new research on topics likely to be of interest to a broad audience and state-of-the-art synthesis and reconsideration pieces that address salient questions and incorporate new data and cases to inform arguments.

Cambridge Elements ≡

American Politics

Elements in the Series

A full series listing is available at: www.cambridge.org/core/series/elements-in-american-politics